It Crossed My Mind by Andrea Hellman
Digital paint, 32 inches by 24 inches. 2023.

Moon City Review
2024

Moon City Review is a publication of Moon City Press, sponsored by the Department of English at Missouri State University, and is distributed by the University of Arkansas Press through the Chicago Distribution Center. Exchange subscriptions with literary magazines are encouraged. The editors of *Moon City Review* contract First North American Serial Rights, all rights reverting to the writers upon publication. The views expressed by authors in *Moon City Review* do not necessarily reflect the opinions of its editors, Moon City Press, or the Department of English at Missouri State University.

Submissions are considered at https://mooncitypress.submittable.com/submit. For more information, please consult www.mooncityreview.com.

Cover art by Andrea Hellman.
Cover designed by Shen Chen Hsieh.
Text copyedited by Karen Craigo.

moon city press
Department of English
Missouri State University

Staff

Table of Contents

Fiction

Nonfiction

Translation

Benjamin S. Grossberg

Pillow Talk With My Octopus Lover

Somehow, we get on the subject
of mothers—I probably
dragged us there—and then
to a particularly grim moment
from late in the chemo.
She's in the front passenger,
barking into a small plastic
trash can, the kind you find
in the corner of a bathroom.
Wasn't really barking, I say,
it just sounded like it, the echo
of her retching in the can.
He's wrapping me tight,
my octopus. He knows
I need it when I get like this.
It's well after midnight;
we're lying abed in the dark.
Tell me, I say, about the rows
of egg sacs, the bursting—
how you launched with
thousands, each of you smaller
than a thimble, how the vast
ocean became the womb
you guys swam in. With a single
sucker, he strokes my hair.
Hair seems to fascinate him:
What in his world is like it?
Do you think about her,

Pillow Talk With My Octopus Lover

I ask, the octopus who laid
those eggs and then stopped
eating, devoting all her energy
to their care? It's not easy
to tell when an octopus
is sad—a wilting of tentacle
or the shush of air leaving
its body .... I nuzzle close
and call him *hatchling*. I think
if he could talk, at moments
like this he'd call me *baby*.

Derek N. Otsuji

Telescoping View of the Last Hawaiian Tree Snail Consumed by Ridge Fire

The illumined blue biome in black space—
        the global ocean's remotest
archipelago—one island in the chain
        of eight—one mountain range of which
one subrange hosts a plant on which
        tree fungus grows, on which one tree snail feeds
—*shell that sounds long*, name for its trilling tongue
        and coy song call to the plover bird
to fetch from fern leaf the forest dew
        —all threatened from beneath when
a mischievous flame, mongoose-like, leaps
        into dry brush. Itching teeth gnaw bark, branch,
bole. An umlaut shrinks into the vowel
        of its shell. The shellac cracks and blackens.

Jessica Goodfellow

Sounds in the Dark

A Foley artist mimics the sound of bones
breaking by snapping celery. For her, bacon
sizzling in a skillet sounds enough like rain.

She advises: A sturdy staple gun can stand in
for gunshots. The crumpling of tinfoil
for thunder, the scrunch of cellophane for fire.

Scientists now say that dark
matter behaves like waves. They know not what
or where it is but can guess at how it undulates.

Pounding a phone book sounds like someone landing
a punch. But who has a phone book these days? Luckily,
hammering a cabbage also does the trick.

The uncertainty principle, too, telling us the more we know
about a particle's speed, the less we know
about its location, and vice versa.

Humans are so human, noticing the brain trying
to make sense the best it can of what is
senseless—helping it along with celery, cellophane, principles.

An arrow on a sound stage can be made to make
a whooshing sound when waved around in a tightly
clenched fist—a thing meant to fly freely, now trapped—

while a pair of leather gloves snapped back and forth
can mimic a bird flapping its wings—*leather* gloves,
wrung from a being never meant to fly.

To produce the plausible sound of a human
heartbeat, flip a trash can upside down.
Push the bottom in and out, in the familiar rhythm.

Some Foley artists prefer a plastic can, while others
use metal, but either way it needs to be
an empty trash can, of course. Empty, meaning full

of dark.

Audra Kerr Brown

How to Bake a Cake in Outer Space

When we pulled the cake from its microgravity oven, it was underdone, a bubbly crater in the middle—not at all how we'd practiced back at Camp Chapawee with balloons tethered to our wrists, a jouncy pile of bunkhouse mattresses beneath our feet. Our Troop Mothers called us to the ship's portholes. *Look,* they said, and we swam over with oven-mitted hands to see Earth, pinned like a merit badge against the black sky. *Look how far you've come.* We thought of the boys from Camp Kachada, how they'd gone to space before us, became Galactic Chefs by roasting hot dogs on the moon. The night before our mission we'd slept on the launchpad, our sleeping bags wagon-wheeled around the campfire. To keep our minds off cracked fuselages and freezing O-rings—off everything that could blow us to biscuits during liftoff—we searched the heavens for constellations. Eighty-eight formations and only three are female: Cassiopeia, Andromeda, and Virgo. Before that, the camp physicians had cracked us open, palpated, prodded, and probed, made sure we were fit for the *rigors of interstellar travel.* They gave us fistfuls of tampons, told us to daisy-chain the strings so they wouldn't break loose and float through the cosmos. We wondered if they could tell who was a virgin, who wasn't. Some parents balked. Feared the solar radiation would mess up their future grandchildren—babies born with hands for feet and blind eyes in belly buttons—so, half our troop was pulled off the project and relegated to the sewing of rickrack along the skirt hems of those still allowed to go. When the head office in Kalamazoo announced that we Camp Chapawee girls would be the first female troop in outer space, we hoped to study neonatal nebula or test the theory of time dilation, but it was determined we'd demonstrate how to bake a cake. At the boys' badge-pinning ceremony, we served crescent sandwiches and star-shaped cookies, watched looped footage of them freewheeling in their tents like socks in a dryer. They showed us moon rocks. They told us space smells like burnt steak. They pinned our shoulders against the knotted pine walls, said, *This is what three Gs feels like*, their penises hard as rockets against our thighs.

Chloe N. Clark

Movement of Constellations

On Mars, I imagine there's so much dust. You can't see it in the air on the screens that broadcast the landing, but I know it's there. My older brother used to tell me that I had a good imagination. I'd talk about places I'd never been, only read about in books, and he said it was like I'd been there, that he could see the places when I described them. In his letters home to us, he wrote of the wet heat and the way it clung to his skin, that the air felt like he was stepping out of a too-long and too-hot shower. "Steam-thick" is how he described it. Years later, when walking in that same country, I felt the air and thought while I had the imagination, my brother had been the one who could tell the truth.

He was double my age that year, which was the kind of math I liked. A brother can only be double the age of his sister once. If he is nine years older, then 18 is that perfect year. He'd spent nine years without me in his life and then nine with me. Addition. I doubled his age at 36. Subtraction.

We'd read all the articles and interviews with the Mercury program and then the Apollo astronauts. Robbie collected the *Life* magazine issues, stacked them in a pile on his desk. He'd rotate which cover was on top. We each had a favorite astronaut. His was Alan Shepard, but I liked Michael Collins. Years later, I remembered a pub trivia night where no one could name the third man involved in the moon landing. Everyone knew Buzz and Neil, but only I whispered Collins under my breath as I sat in the corner away from the bustle.

The truth about having your brother die when you are nine is that you never really knew who he was. You didn't get to grow up and see the way his life unfolded, find out how he was away from his childhood home. Maybe we'd have grown apart, have called only a couple times a year. Maybe we'd have hated each other, but we never got the chance.

If you asked me why I worked in space, I'd've said I was always interested. And I was, but my interest was born in Robbie reading those *Life* magazines with me, us watching every news program that talked to astronauts. When I worked in operations, there weren't that many woman flight controllers. Enough we all could raise a cheer for Sally Ride, but not enough that it didn't make the photos look like a Boy Scout reunion. I thought Robbie could have been one of them. Maybe we'd work together; maybe I would have done something different then. Maybe he'd've pointed to a picture of Sally then to me, said that could be you.

The truth is I worked in the space industry because I wanted to understand.

My brother died on the same day we landed men on the moon for the first time. Or that's what I tell people if they ask, though really it was just the day we were informed. Likely, he died days earlier. The news processed through various departments until it found its way to my parents' door. Soldiers. A gold star. Folded flag. Years later, when I tell the story, it feels like a punch line rather than something that happened to us.

But, on July 20 in 1969, it was only ours. A sunny day and someone knocked on the door. I answered, because at nine I still got excited when someone knocked in case it was a package, a letter just for me. Robbie's letters had started happening less so after the first couple of months. Years later, I'd wondered if it was because the more that he saw the less that he had to say.

The men at the door wore suits, pins on their lapel. They looked official, serious. I thought maybe they were going to tell us that Robbie was coming home. The war had ended and they were personally coming to tell every family the good news. How exciting that would have been, to be the one informing, and see such joy over and over.

My mom had come out from the kitchen to see who I was talking to, and her expression shifted so suddenly. I felt my tummy drop, like when the Ferris wheel reached its peak, and I always worried, for just a second, that we'd stop and never get down.

"Thomas!" she yelled to my father. He popped out of his study so quickly that it was like he'd been waiting. Maybe he'd been waiting from the moment Robbie left. His own brother had died in World War II, though, they'd both been soldiers then. Maybe that made it better, the knowing how terrible it was that the worst felt like relief, like you were no longer waiting.

The men asked my mother to sit down, a practiced gesture, though it was my father whose legs gave out, who fell to the ground. They had wanted me to go play in another room, but my mother had put a hand on my shoulder. The same motion she made when adults had talked about serious things—the neighbor girl who ran off with some boy from out of town, their fears of the war—and had expected her to send me from the room. My parents had always wanted me to hear everything, to take it all in.

Robbie was nine years older, but he'd push me on the swing. He'd say, Here you're going to outer space, to Mars. When I was at the highest, he'd tell me to jump. I'd close my eyes and feel the air rush around me, my hair flying up behind me. The weightless weight of falling.

And he always caught me.

The truth is: I don't remember where Robbie died. I'm sure they said, some place name, some battle. The truth is: I can't unremember the sound of my father hitting the ground, the way my mother never broke eye contact with the man telling her.

We watched the moon landing that night, my father insistent. Later he said he wanted to see it go right, to see three men live against the weight of odds and endless space. But, in the moment, we watched through tears, through that expanse of dark. Around the world, people cheered from the edges of their seats.

When we land on Mars, all those decades and decades and decades later, when the first person steps out into the planet we could only imagine for so long, everyone will be watching. Feet on surface. All those giant leaps.

I wonder what he was thinking about all that time marching through woods and heat. Did he imagine outer space or some other dream? Did he think about the Apollo mission and wonder if we'd make it?

Avitus B. Carle

Close: A Father/Daughter Breakup Defined

Close (adj): a short distance away

We break up over a Wendy's salad. At least, that's what this feels like, a breakup. I guess fathers can't break up with their daughters. You say things like *Your mother and I* and *It's over* and *You'll be better off* and *I love you, kiddo*. The tips of our shoes touch under the table. We pull soggy lettuce from our mouths at the same time, wipe our damp hands on the thighs of our jeans. *See ya*, you say, and I want to believe you. But I can't. Because you step on my foot before you leave. Because you've already forgotten you're my ride home.

Close (adj): carefully guarded

I remember you in fragments so I can pick and choose what to forget. Like when I'm eight and witness you arguing with Mom for the first time. Mom on one side of your bed saying she goes out because you've stopped shaving. You on the side where her imprint evaporated three months prior and relocated to the couch. You stopped shaving because she stopped noticing. She only sees the worst in you. You only berate the best version of her. I wonder where these two versions live. I wonder if either of them has time to tuck me in and whisper good night.

Close (adv): in a position so as to be very near to someone or something; with very little space between

Before you leave, but after you stop tucking me in, you teach me about love and all its failures. We are at the Ferris wheel's peak when you say

I loved you, once. I ask if you still love me. You talk about how love can be felt for so many useless things. I ask if you still love me. You talk about loving the view. I ask if you still love me. You talk about cheesesteaks and Wendy's salads. Watching icicles melt on the gutter. But do you love me? I move closer until our arms intertwine. Until our legs twist, my foot resting on yours. Dad? Dad, you say, three letters, nothing more. Just like love, you say, as we begin our descent. Just four letters, bookended by an "L" and "e." Nothing more.

Close (adj): denoting a family member who is part of a person's immediate family, typically a parent or sibling

You were the only one who didn't make fun of me for watching *Land Before Time*. I was nine and changed my name to Little Foot, walking on all fours. You picked tree stars for me from the tallest cabinet, from the top of the fridge. I was ten watching *Clifford: The Big Red Dog*, lapping chicken noodle soup from a bowl. You called me your good girl between the ages of twelve and thirteen. At fourteen, you tucked me in for the last time. You read *The Little Engine That Could*, your breath smelling like pine cones after it rains.

Close (v): move or cause to move so as to cover an opening

After you leave, I pack what remains into cardboard boxes. I use masking tape. I write the names of rooms I imagine your new house contains. Office. Den. Pantry. All in Sharpie, with maps for where each item should be. In a box marked "kitchen" I write an apology for the absence of all your plates. Mom threw them at the trash collectors. They refused to take the only box she packed. The one containing your marriage license and all the half-torn photos of you. She forgets about the worst of you. Only sees the worst in me. We talk around each other without you. Her having conversations with lamps and light bulbs, waiting for me to leave, too. Me, talking to all the doors and windows, wanting to leave, knowing I need to stay.

Close (n): the end of an event or of a period of time or activity

Six months and you still haven't come. Your boxes remain by the door. There are bills and empty cabinets. There is mom watching *Wheel of Fortune*. I miss the sight of boiling water. I miss smoke rising from a pot. I miss pine cones and *Clifford* and tree stars. I miss the sound of you pressing microwave buttons. I apply to five Wendy's in the area. Get hired at three. Work at two. The one closest to Mom who blames me for destroying her body. Who blames me for her loneliness and everything she hates about you. The one where I last saw you, where I make sure the lettuce leaves are never soggy.

Close (v): bring or come to an end

I find out you're married again through Facebook. Your wife looks like Mom. Despite the wig. Despite her crooked teeth. Despite the way you rest your hands on her stomach. I know I won't hear from you. I know I'll never see you again. Still, I want you to know, I'm waiting for you at Wendy's. I'm a grill cook at the one closest to Mom. I work the window at the Wendy's where I last saw you. I imagine your voice through the speaker in the winter. I ask for your order. You tell me about love. How it hurts. How it breaks. How it dissipates when we least expect it. When the window peels open and I see someone else's father, I still try to imagine they're you. I wonder, if I asked, would they tell me they loved me? Or, was this all just a four-letter word, nothing more?

Avitus B. Carle

Seaworthy

After the storm and before our parents stir from their beds, we race to the beach to see what's washed ashore. Wooden arms bent at their elbows. Glass eyes with cracked pupils. Metal legs we use to point at metal plates that—we assume—belong to the skulls where the seagulls perch. We wave our discoveries in the air, chase the seagulls into flight with our songs, until our voices catch and defuse in our throats when we notice the size of the skulls. They remind us of our parents' heads without skin, without smiles, without who we've just left behind. One of us suggests that this is what happens when adults venture into the sea. We gather what's left of the limbs and eyes, but not the skulls, which we place the steel plates on like hats, believing that the skulls on the beach should be left to wait for the rest of their remains to float ashore. We bury the limbs and the eyes in our parents' closets, sock drawers, beneath the driver's seats in their cars, believing that the remains of others will be enough to protect them from the next incoming storm.

Quentin Parker

Boiling Point

I spend the beginning of our last day entranced by the sky. Streaks of yellows and golds, occasional flares of bright-hot oranges and reds.

Ed grumbles from the bedroom door, "The walls are warmer today. Sun's bigger. Shouldn't be long now." He scratches at a newly forming sun blister on his cheek. I tell him to keep away from the outside air, but he swears up and down this bunker is depleting in oxygen by the minute. He may well be right; I would kill for a cold breeze.

"I don't wanna talk about that," I say, my attention stolen once again by the fiery sky beyond our tinted viewing window. The world never told us why the sun had widened or why its white light darkened into a blood-orange sphere. It menaces over what life is left to view it.

"I sure as hell hope it's quick."

"How much longer?" Dominic whines, one fist an iron grip on my shoulder from the back seat, the other bunching his pants between his legs. "I gotta pee!"

Patience, evidently, is a virtue I continue to grapple with well into adulthood. The drive to Yellowstone is long and arduous, albeit we would be an hour ahead had Dom packed the night before like I told him to and if Ed hadn't wasted time arguing against the trip. Dom has been incapable of sitting still for the past four hours. He needs to move constantly, to switch positions, to ask someone about something he spent less than five minutes of thought on. He is an erratic energy in a directionless frame. It keeps my days interesting.

My husband side-eyes me in distaste of this completely avoidable situation. He's a sit-by-the-local-lake kind of man, staunchly opposed to endless, droning road trips—even more so with a hyperactive child in tow. We lost the lakes, then the rivers, and a few yards of ocean not long after the change. Regardless, the calming energy of a serene body of water could do nothing to penetrate Dom's attention.

"We've got an hour and a half left, buddy. Do you think you can make it?" Ed asks.

I see our kid eye my empty coffee cup in the rearview mirror.

Ed and I look at each other. He huffs and gestures to hand the cup over. "Make sure you take the lid off this time, Dom."

Beads of sweat form along my hairline and knees. The temperature in the bunker is a few degrees higher—not enough to put us out of our misery, as it is. I sit beside my half of Dom's pile and rummage through the bottom for something cool. I settle for pressing his tennis shoes against my forehead.

When Dom's first sunspot appeared, it came with seven more within the day. That week, they spread from ankle to thigh and wrist to collarbone. In less than a month, he was unrecognizable. His skin darkened with the sun. He stopped leaving his room and tossed his belongings into the hallway. I kept them as a close collection in case he'd want them back. In case this would all be over soon. I caught him stealing looks at the sky through his shielded viewing window, as if he expected to soon be lifted into the fire.

I tried my best to recount his convoluted sandwich and soup recipes on the days he couldn't get himself out of bed. He always functioned best with minimal ingredients and limited parental supervision. He could barely eat by this point, no more than we could stomach it, either.

"I can toss it!"

"No!"

The full cup bobs in Dom's hand as he throws yet another tantrum. I long for the age when he learns rational thought. Moving car means wind, which means splash-back, which means pulling over on one of the projected hottest days yet to clean his piss off the seats.

When planning the trip, Ed was wary of stopping anywhere that led to us being outside longer than what was absolutely necessary. The night before, he tried to settle on watching the geysers from the car window, and I threatened to lock him out for an hour. Dom's sunspots are bad enough; the sunscreen no longer soothes the itches and burns, and further exposure will only expedite the process.

I know this.

Dom begged to see the hot springs before the sun could take him. Even on his most painful days, he could never see the reasoning for why we stayed indoors. Today, we needed to indulge him on his wish. He may not get to the age when he knows to eat with his mouth closed and color within the lines rather than on the walls. We can hold his hand until it hardens to stone, but he deserves this, even if it means facing the splash-back to keep from lingering outside for too long.

For the time being in the car, we let him know that Santa doesn't like kids who toss their piss out of car windows.

A month after the sun changed, water no longer stayed cold. Our freezer thawed and rotted what fresh food we had left in a matter of days. Ed was quick in his decision to broker a deal with our next-door neighbors. In exchange for Dom's pillows and mattress, we could get their extra minifreezer.

I throw myself in front of the door, no matter how badly the rippling heat scorches the backs of my arms.

"G'dammit, move!" he yells.

"No. We keep it, or you go with it."

"You give me the photo and his shoes, and it's yours."

I glance between our two halves of the pile. Ed already has Dom's trophies, his macaroni necklace, his stuffed dragon, his third favorite shirt. I never got that stuffed dragon back from him, and it would be no different with his shoes. The photo, especially, stays with me.

"They're mine."

"Then move."

I claw for the opposite corners of the mattress, and for an hour we fight, insult each other in every way we know will sting, then drop it and wrestle for the pillows. I scratch at his face, he pulls my hair, we tangle in a mess of frantic limbs in primal desperation. The heat leaves me drowning in sweat and rendered near unconscious from exhaustion, and by the time I'm coherent enough to sit up, Dom's bedding is gone. As if he never had a place here.

We keep the minifreezer in the darkest corner of the bunker, away from the doors and windows. The heat still bleeds through the insulation and into our remaining food and water stores.

I ask Ed if he thinks it was worth it. He flips me off.

He knows it wouldn't help, of course. A part of me couldn't stand to look at Dom's deathbed, either.

Dom shrieks each time a geyser erupts, somehow even louder than the pillar of scalding water. It concerns me that he can't tell the difference between boiling water rocketing a hundred feet in the air and the fountains at the local water park. Ed and I have to explain to him twice why he can't go play in the hot spring.

The water gives way to billowing steam. I instinctually flinch away from the heat, but as the mist graces our skin, I feel a bit of the childish joy that Dom so relentlessly expresses at any given moment. I let myself crack a ghost of a smile then give in to a giggle, and our son gazes at me with the same wonder as he does the geysers.

The sun peers just above the mountains, and I see its rising tangerine eye for the first time today. The sweltering celestial body is watchful. Gleaming. It eradicated the night and yet lets us bathe in its gentle warmth for the time being. I try to promise this same warmth for life to Dom, even when he wriggles free of our grasp to dig in the yard for roly-polies and earthworms. I angle my camera to capture his blackened hands grasping the railing, a geyser jumping up in front of him as the morning glow wraps his skin in a loving orange. The sunspots haven't crawled past his collar yet, and it's the widest I've seen him smile.

The ride home is silent. He's seen all that he needs to see.

Ed's blister spreads and hardens into another black sunspot. It's identical to the ones that inch up my forearms and to the ones that sprouted on his back after Dom left us. I slap his hand away from the wound; otherwise it'll bleed.

"Shit!" he exclaims.

"I told you to stop doing that."

"What does it matter, anyway?"

"Shut up, Ed."

"They aren't gonna stop growing. You gotta accept that."

"Shut up!"

Ed frowns and turns his back to me. "You weren't crazy like this before."

"I have a right to be!" I scream. "I'm trapped in a fucking oven! You won't stop letting heat in, my arms burn, and my scalp is dry, and

I hate taking cold showers, but I can't now because there's no such thing as cold anymore, and our boy's bed is gone—"

"I knew you were still worked up over that. You could've had it if you just shared."

"Why, so you can give it away for something useless again?"

"At least I tried something! You sit next to your pile and act like you're dead with him. What else do you want from me?"

I sit beside my half of Dom's things, and Ed sits with his. With stiffened hands, I manage to pluck the photo of Dom from inside his old tee-ball helmet. I can't tell if the mist I feel on my cheeks are tears or the fleeting memory of Yellowstone leaving my body with the last of the moisture I had left. Another offering to the sun.

"Our kid is gone, Ed," I say, barely above a whisper. "And you smell like shit."

His head lolls along the wall until his eyes meet mine. "I know. That's the most you've said to me all week."

"I know."

At some point in my daze, Ed crawled across the bunker to sit beside me. I feel the back of his hand graze my arm, mindful of the creeping sunspots. Beams of red from the noon sky pool as the sun peaks, bathing the bunker in radiant, bloody crimson. I can hear the crackling of what's left of the greenery being eaten by flame, reduced to kindling. Waves of heat dance across my vision, and I let my hand with the photo fall limp between us. Ed scoops up the photo with a small smile, and I grimace. Its edges fray brown from the air, and in the exchange my husband's skin burns like Dominic's.

"Where do you think we'll go?" I ask.

"The sun made up its mind about us. Hopefully, it takes us to our boy. We can't keep ourselves away for much longer."

No one else has been able to.

Ed shoulders the wall and pushes himself to his feet. I squint through the light at his outstretched hand and take it, suddenly on my feet. The photo of Dom remains pressed between us as we embrace. We stand there, swaying weakly in the middle of the bunker, almost in a dance.

I wonder if Dom knew like we do that this is our end day. Stabbing light cuts through the cracks in the exit door, behind it the remnants of our charring atmosphere. Ed leans his head on top of mine, the only thing keeping me on my feet being the dwindling strength left in his arms. As we sway, I hope we leave slowly enough to feel the warmth of Dominic on this Earth before the red giant in the sky takes us to him.

Dane Slutzky

Fortune

Venus was in retrograde, the days waxing
on & off. My nails burned down to their nail beds,
the candles burned down to their wick's end,
the oceans drained to wherever oceans go.

That's weather, not climate. I rolled the dice,
snake eyes. I drew a card—it told me to stock up
on reserves before the dark night of the soul.
I bought Under Armour and seed bombs.

I bought nut milk fortified with vitamins.
Fortification was what I needed, becoming a stronghold—
all that gold in my chest with a moat. I read the script,
I knew the adventure would end at the beginning,

the journey was the prize, etc. & so forth. I bought
a one-way ticket. When the storm cleared, I ran.

Dane Slutzky

Aesthetics

We're cottage core we're goblin mode
we'll use the same water glass each meal
tracking in dirt and embroidering dirt
and oiling our boots once a year.
Wait until the snow has melted, see you
in the spring. Gathering mushrooms in
a basket, unsure which are safe to eat.
Don't throw away the vegetables—we're
recording their decay: landscapes
of rot, blossoms of mold, spore
prints over the counter. Homes for the
flies that crawl inside. We light fires
and yell into the night. We're coyotes,
fisher cats. We have found a cave.
Tracking in ice that melts in puddles
to reflect our innermost selves. We're one
facet of the crystal that refracts the beams
of light. We're stirring the mixture
widdershins in a gyre. Planets
perambulate the sky as we bury
a goat's horn stuffed
with quartz.

Daphne Daugherty

The Day the Two Dogs Killed the Second Chicken, My Father Took Them for a Walk in the Woods.

I wonder which one he killed second,
which one heard the gunshot, which one
spent his last few moments cowering,
tail down, confusion setting in, the scent
of blood swirling around him, dog blood
instead of bird but blood all the same.
I wonder if he tried to run. I wonder
if he could hear the chickens from there,
from the clearing in the woods
where dogs go to die. I wonder
if it matters that if he had looked up
he would have seen my father
with tears in his eyes, an empty bottle
of vodka by his feet to get him through.

Daphne Daugherty

Conjure

You know what to do: gather mushrooms.
Oysters and turkey tails and fly agaric,
whatever you find in the woods.
Check the Farmer's Almanac
for moon cycles and the best time
to plant tomatoes, the best time
to look for lemon balm and hellebore
and Arkansas ginseng. Prepare.
This is blood magic, root magic, magic
like they used to do before Golgotha
before Chichen Itza before sacrifices
were to gods, back when they were
to the spirits and the spirits returned
the favor. Back when these Ozark hills
were real mountains, huge craggy spires
reaching to the clouds. Don't ask
for love. You won't get it. Only ask
for what the spirits will give. Rain.
Starlight. The tails of chipmunks
spat out by house cats. Things
you need to fight back the dark.

Sarah L. Sassone

The Matriarch

After my wife, Annie, died, our elephant Polly mourned her for five months before returning to her herd on the conservation in Mali. In the next few days, the rest of her family—her own mate, sisters and brothers, children—slowly wandered away from us, but Polly sat by Annie's grave every day, her trunk stroking the tombstone.

In the last month of Annie's life, when the cancer engulfed her, Polly waited outside our bedroom window, her trunk available for hand-holding. Annie asked me to compile hundreds of pounds of vegetation for Polly to make sure she still ate—because some of us don't eat when distraught—and to encourage her, Annie and I ate with her. I cooked food that didn't repulse Annie, like soup and pasta, and fed it to her when she was too weak to hold a spoon. Polly lifted food with her trunk and scooped it into her mouth, although sometimes she tried to feed it to Annie. Each night, Annie told me, "Please still tend to all the elephants when I'm gone. Especially Polly."

When Annie died, Polly called her herd over to our house on the day of the funeral to join the dozens of friends and family who had flown to Africa to pay respects to my wife. Polly stood beside me, and I saw drops fall to the ground from her small eyes. It was more rain than we got all year.

For five long, hot desert months, I made sure to keep Polly healthy. I loaded my truck with cut-down trees and roots, bought international fruit at the closest supermarket thirty miles away, and pulled as much grass as I could find. Sometimes, I slept beside Polly at night, next to Annie's grave. But, after five months, I couldn't take it anymore.

"Polly," I said, stroking her trunk and leading her away from my wife. "It's my turn." She looked away, but in the morning, she was gone.

Melissa Llanes Brownlee

Regret

It's dark and cool. Lights are flashing in the ceiling. There's a gravestone in front of you. You read Michael Myers and feel thunder shake your young body. You aren't scared. You look down and there is no ground under the rickety walkway, just black goop, and you think it's probably blood.

You regret asking the waiter for real rice at the Chinese restaurant your auntie took you to when they placed white rice on the lazy Susan and it wasn't sticky but fluffy, an array of gravy-covered egg foo yong, thin slices of char siu, beef broccoli, surrounding it. You beg for ketchup and shoyu, and your auntie laughs as you bow your head in shame.

You regret getting lost with your sister in Knott's Berry Farm when your auntie specifically told you to meet everyone at the fried chicken restaurant out front by six but you were having too much fun, riding the Corkscrew and pretending you were weightless on the Parachute Sky Jump, your slippers scrunched between your toes so they wouldn't fly off as you dangled in the sky. She pulls your ear hard when you finally meet them. You try not to cry and you want to bow your head, shamed.

You regret digging a bobby pin in your ears when flying from Hawai'i because it didn't help them pop, not knowing that all you needed was a stick of Doublemint or Big Red and you'd be feeling better in no time. Your auntie tries to smack some sense into you, your head as sore as your ears, and you hide your head in shame as the stewardess looks away.

You regret not riding Space Mountain more than two times, the darkness, welcoming and inviting, the lights, stars and galaxies you dream of visiting, the music sending chills through your little body. Your blood sings as you exit the ride each time. The second time your auntie screams at you to move your ass or you will miss the parade, and you shake your head, looking around, ashamed of her.

You regret not knowing how to pray when you are with the auntie and uncle and the cousins in the hotel room at night before bed, the words flowing so easily from their tongues. You sheepishly say God is love and bow your head to hide your shame.

You close your eyes and worry that it will make it worse, your auntie behind you as you walk through the Halloween exhibit at the Hollywood Wax Museum. You take a deep breath, knowing that even wax could come alive and get you, exiting into the *Nightmare on Elm Street*, Freddy's finger-knives hovering, and you tell yourself, you regret nothing.

Lori D'Angelo

Lift Me Up, Drag Me Down

The near-death experiences you hear about on TV talk shows are the nice ones. The ones with angels and comforting white light and long-loved, long-missed dead relatives. Maybe throw in a harp or two and a street of gold. They're the kind of experiences you want to write down and go on speaking tours about because they're so encouraging. The message of them all is basically the same: It gets better. You're not alone. Everything has a purpose. God has a plan.

But my experience of dying was nothing like that. When I died, I went to hell. As you can expect, it was not pleasant. I suppose you'll be wanting details. In this age of online everything, everyone wants details, and preferably selfies.

Thankfully, I have no hell selfies, and I wouldn't post them if I did. Social media is mostly us sharing with other people the life we want to have, not the one we actually do. If not a play for my life is the best, we make a play for my life is the worst. I'm poorer, sadder, more alone than the rest of you saps.

In hell, you don't get any sympathy, and everyone is too busy enduring the misery of their own pain to compare it to yours.

Which is worse? Death by fire or death by water? No one cares. They're both pretty horrible, and, whatever your hell is, you relive it again and again and again.

My hell was being trapped in the kitchen with Toby that night he pushed me down and laughed and laughed. I was bleeding. He was sorry. Drunk was his excuse. Couldn't he see how crazy I made him? The things I made him do. The broken plates. The bashed-in doors. The cabinets ripped off hinges. Me wanting to say something other than please just stop but not knowing what.

They told me they found me on the side of the road amid some grass and weeds and other trash. Someone left me there.

You're lucky, they said, to be alive. Was there anyone they could call?

They looked clean and blessed and purified like they wouldn't understand my hell even if I took them there and walked them through. When it's not your hell, you don't understand how a person is trapped, how that person could ever stay.

I shook my head. No, I said there's no one. But did they have more of that fine banana pudding and a Bible?

They look pleased, and I felt like maybe, if I tried harder, I could have a life filled with church potlucks and women's circles and a Jesus who saved me. I wanted that. If I had an urge to see Toby, all I had to do was go back to hell.

Mary Grimm

Dead Boyfriends

On one of those hot afternoons, my sister and I had a discussion about our dead boyfriends, although she argued that we should call them dead lovers, since boyfriends sounded juvenile. The question was how many there were. We knew of three, two of mine and one of hers, but, given our age, surely there were more.

The heat was oppressive, the kind that you feel like a blanket on your skin, a blanket of air fitted closely to you. In a heat like that you bake but don't sweat. The bees were languid. The drops of condensation on our glasses moved slowly downward. We were drinking old fashioneds with a slew of cherries.

You remember the one who had a parrot, she said. I said yes. He was dead for sure, years ago, but had it been a car accident? We weren't certain. My sister had gone to a party with him and left with someone else, dashing his hopes forever. It wasn't the sort of thing she did usually. He hadn't protested when she left with the man she later married and, still later, divorced. Didn't he say anything at all? I asked. But she couldn't remember. Well, make something up for me, I said. Give me a good story.

Hmmm, she said, looking to the sky, which was flat and blue and lowering, for inspiration. He begged you not to go? I prompted. He tried to throw a punch? He'd never do that, she said, which was true. He'd been mild, mild-mannered, quiet, undemanding, his parrot the only colorful thing about him.

If he was still alive, I said, we could ask him. We could find him on Facebook and message him and find out what he remembered. Like, say, Johnboy, what was going through your mind when your date walked out the door with your nemesis? Did you go home and cry about it with your parrot?

Now you're just being mean, my sister said, which was true. But sometimes meanness is good for you. It's hygienic, in a way, something that cuts down and through.

What about your dead boyfriends, she said. Are you going to FB message them with a Q and A? What about that one whose father was a minister? Oh, him, I said.

I had only found out that he was dead a few months before. He wasn't Facebook findable, and I googled here and there until I found his obituary. Not only was he dead, but he'd been dead for almost ten years. Ten years during which I'd thought of him occasionally, sometimes with affection, sometimes with guilt (because I'd broken up with him rather abruptly), remembering especially that one time we'd had in his single bed, in a hurry before one of his parents came back. Out the window, if we'd looked, we could see the church steeple, like a New England postcard. But all this time, he'd been dead.

He had been a minister himself when he died, and therefore I suppose that he expected to go to some version of heaven. He must have expected to be able to look down on his wife and children and parishioners from wherever he was, maybe on people he'd known in the past. Maybe he had the sort of death where you revisit your past life.

I told all this to my sister and she said, rather cuttingly, did you hope he was thinking of you?

Of course not, I said.

But it would have been nice if he had.

John Jodzio

Hot Ghost

Hot Ghost first visited Lanie when her boyfriend Charles was at a week-long medical device conference. Lanie was half asleep, and at first thought Hot Ghost was just a regular ghost—doughy and prone to whining. She almost told him to get the fuck out of her bedroom, but then she saw he was in his mid-twenties with a good ghost haircut and a taut ghost stomach and a bluish aura surrounding his body instead of the normal, boring green one.

"How'd you die?" Lanie asked.

This was the first thing Lanie always asked ghosts. It wasn't the most appropriate or delicate thing she could've asked, but she usually asked it in a playful way, and most of them, except the Civil War ghosts, never seemed to mind.

"I was running an ultramarathon, and a tree fell on me," Hot Ghost said.

"Yow," Lanie said. "Bad luck."

Hot Ghost shrugged. "At least it wasn't a heart attack or some boring bullshit like that."

Lanie had fucked ghosts before. It was just innocent fun, a perk of living in an older Victorian or near a graveyard. It would have been something fun to talk about at a brunch or happy hour, maybe with her old college roommates, if all of them weren't so busy or so angry at her, or maybe with her former work friends, if they hadn't all gotten so preachy. All of her old friends had gotten so angry and so busy and so preachy lately that Lanie had gone to brunch alone the day before and sat at a table, scrolling through her phone and drinking endless mimosas and not getting to brag about all the excellent ghost dick she was getting.

"Do you wanna make out?" Lanie asked Hot Ghost.

"Sure," he nodded. "I'd be down for that."

Lanie watched as he floated across the room, toward her bed. Most of the ghosts she'd slept with so far had thinning hair, but Hot Ghost had a full head of thick hair and a tan that made his teeth seem incredibly white.

"Do you want to know my name?" Hot Ghost said, pulling his tank top over his head.

"Fuck no," Lanie said.

The next night, Lanie was emptying her dishwasher when Hot Ghost floated through her kitchen wall. He leaned on her granite countertop, near the energy bar that she was planning to eat even though she knew it would only make her more exhausted than she already was.

"I think I forgot my ring here last night," Hot Ghost said. "I took it off and set it down on your nightstand and forgot to grab it when I left."

Ugh. Usually, ghosts didn't pull this kind of sophomoric bullshit, but Lanie was pretty good at ghost sex, so every once in a while, one of them glommed on, thinking that there might be some sort of interdimensional future between the two of them.

"You weren't wearing a ring," Lanie said.

Hot Ghost was wearing the same clothes as the night before: the running shorts, the tank top. This was one of the things Lanie hated about ghosts, how they always had on the same outfits they were wearing when they died.

"Fine," Hot Ghost said. "I didn't leave anything here. I just wanted to see you again."

Lanie grabbed the silverware out of the dishwasher. Hot Ghost was in her way, and she took a handful of forks and stuck them through his stomach and into the drawer. He said "ouch" in a jokey way, but Lanie didn't laugh, because she noticed her pill case on the kitchen counter behind Hot Ghost and she wondered if she'd thrown away the correct number of pills the night before. She opened the case and counted again. She opened up the garbage can and ruffled the bag to make sure she hadn't accidentally left them in there again. The last time Charles had come home from a medical device conference, all the pills she was supposed to take were sitting right there at the top of the garbage bag, the shiny ones and the salmon-colored ones and those giant ones that were hard to swallow, which was so, so dumb of her, and Charles pointed them out to Lanie and she panicked, told him she did not know whose pills those were, that while they might look like her pills, they were for damn sure not her pills because she had taken all her fucking pills, they were probably some of her work friends' pills because some work friends had popped by the night before and they'd probably tossed their pills in the garbage at some point? Probably Cynthia or Lisa? Maybe Kathryn? If he was so concerned, she could ask everyone at work the next day to see who'd done the pill tossing? And if it was such a giant deal to him, she guessed she could text them right then, even though it was pretty late and they probably wouldn't answer? And Charles said that wasn't necessary, that it was OK, to just forget about it. She'd felt so guilty about the pill-tossing that for the last three months she'd made sure Charles was always around when she swallowed her pills, and after she downed them she would open her mouth and lift up her tongue, slide it up and down and over and around and say, Ahhh, ahhhh, show him her empty mouth like she was in some psych ward and could not be trusted.

"We were a one-time thing," Lanie told Hot Ghost now. "There's nothing more for you here."

Hot Ghost's face scrunched in a way that made him look like a banshee. It was obvious he was used to getting whatever he wanted, both alive and dead, and it pissed Lanie off that he thought he could just barge in here and fuck up her whole day. Charles would be home soon, and she needed to check the bathroom again for stray pills. She had flushed them down the toilet this time, but all of that pill-throwing happened in non-optimal-pill-disposing light, and she thought maybe she'd dropped one of them and heard it skitter under the bathroom sink, and even though she'd gotten down on her hands and knees and patted down every square inch of the bathroom floor multiple times, she could not get that clickety-clack sound of a pill landing on ceramic tile out of her head.

"Could you slide back into the floor joists or go jump back into the water heater?" Lanie asked Hot Ghost. "Could you return to wherever you live and don't come back here again?"

"Jesus," Hot Ghost said, holding up his palms and backing away. "No problem."

☾

Charles got home from his medical device conference, and Lanie greeted him with a kiss. After she kissed him, a plate flew from the kitchen and shattered against the wall. Then another. While more plates flew and shattered, there was some loud moaning that sounded partly sexual and partly scary. Lanie ducked under the dining room table to protect herself, but Charles stood there, not ducking or flinching at all.

"Are you seeing something?" he asked.

She only wanted to take a break from the pills for like a week to see what would happen, to see if her brain would quit buzzing and to see if her hands would be less shaky and to see if she could write a text or an email that didn't have an exclamation point in it. She wanted to be able to drink three or four mimosas without feeling like she was going to puke, but now Charles was looking at her through the gap in the tablecloth in the way Lanie hated, kindhearted and soft-eyed, a look that always made her feel like she was weak and sick and failing.

A picture from when Charles and Lanie went swimming with dolphins in Florida shot across the room and smashed against the wall. Old-school ghosts had discretion, Lanie thought, but these newer ones had no fucking chill whatsoever. A glass vase flew across the dining room and broke against the wall. She'd fucked the wrong ghost, and now she needed to deal with the fallout.

"I need to tell you the truth," Lanie said. "I slept with a ghost this weekend."

Lanie thought after she said this, Charles might yell at her, stomp around, call her names, storm out, but he stood there and nodded at her, said, OK, sure, OK. Maybe his anger would come later on, maybe passive-aggressively? Maybe some anger would finally burst out of his body, and he would punch a hole in a door or wall. She wanted him to do something like that just one time. She wanted him to come unglued, unhinged. She wanted something different than kindness and understanding.

"Didn't you hear me?" Lanie asked. "About the ghost-fucking?"

"We fixed this last time, and we can fix it again," Charles said.

After Charles said this, all of Hot Ghost's moaning and plate-breaking stopped. Sometimes, Charles said the exact right thing that made a ghost disappear. It was a difficult thing to find in a boyfriend but not impossible.

"Should I call Sara?" he asked.

Sara was Lanie's younger sister. The last time she came to help, she'd taken off work, stayed for ten days. Lanie slept through most of her visit, but whenever she would wake up, she would hear Sara and Charles chatting downstairs, and when Sara left, she and Charles hugged for what seemed like too much time. Over the last few months, she'd told herself that there was no reason for her not to trust either of them, but now Lanie knew she had been mistaken.

"When was the last time you saw Sara?" she asked Charles. "Did she come meet you at your conference?"

If Charles had cheated on her with her sister, that would be unforgivable. She'd go on a ghost-sex spree if that happened, get her revenge. Whenever she'd have revenge sex with any of these ghosts, she'd make them stay late into the night, venting about Charles and Sara and the awful betrayal that ripped her whole family apart.

Lanie was still sitting under the table, and Charles was still holding out his hand.

"It will be OK," he said.

Charles would leave soon. Maybe in a few weeks. Maybe a few months. At most, they had another year. Lanie wouldn't blame him when he left. It was fine. It was OK. She'd be fine without him. Nobody stayed for long.

Marcy Rae Henry

the mammal that has the longest orgasm

first thing to do before moving is to take stock
toss socks, eat all the food, and light as many fires as you can
because you may not have another fireplace
and because burning is more fun than shredding

midwestern wood, wet and aging like cheese,
takes forever to light
but my last apartment in albuquerque caught fire
without anyone trying

first thing to do before moving in with someone
is not to talk about sums or money or psalms
we slept together before living together—and after
everything in between was fights and fondue
but truly, living with O. was counting black sheep at night

with orgasms between thirty and ninety minutes
the sus scrofa domesticus is not just any pig
O. claimed that if someone had a thirty-minute orgasm
they'd want to commit suicide afterwards

now, moving means i put the sky in a box
countless pairs of sight and sun glasses
then a model of the city where nothing looks dangerous
i put mirrors in a box
pink salt lamps
a gramophone O. gifted me on my thirtieth birthday
and my great-grandparents' naturalization papers

☾

too many euphemisms for death
the mammal with the longest orgasm
is not necessarily the happiest
in the echo of empty walls painted white
i light a cigarette just to have something burning

Jeremy Radin

Donkey Beauty

Now I have a great big gray coat
that makes me feel like a Russian
who stands before a donkey & weeps,
bewildered by the donkey beauty,
though I haven't wept in years—&
when I tell my friends this they look
at me as if I'd told them I've not made
love in years—& when I tell them
I've not made love in years,
they don't look at me at all—
so I've learned to look at myself
& now I've solved self-looking.
It's time to seek new astonishments.
Not only a coat, but warm, sturdy
boots, gloves, a green umbrella
with a curved wooden handle
I twirl as I travel through town.
Though sometimes, I do admit,
I like to stand nude in the rain,
barefoot, without my protections,
& try to feel how I felt that morning,
you know the one—I walked into
my dad's room & found him in bed,
dead as the Romanov dynasty, blue
light leaking out of his hair. I wept
there, in the father beauty, death
beauty, morning beauty. & then
I loved myself. Half-orphan, lost

in the donkey snow, shivering,
I loved myself, I had no choice,
hair turning whiter in the new,
the astonishing cold.

Jeremy Radin

The Mountain

No thank you, I will not be the infant
of your life, I will be, thank you, the mountain.
& in the morning, when the sun rises
in the sky like an enormous blue someone
with an impossibly bright
little asshole getting up from the toilet,
you will say my God, look at that mountain,
and you will say it about me,
the mountain of your life, not the infant,
as once I was, the infant who needed
something from you—a graham cracker
or your tissue-wrapped hand gathering
my greenyellow filth, no, I will very extremely be
the mountain, & you will kneel
at my foot with your fists full of grass,
weeping, thanking God for all of that suffering
because it gave you an opportunity
to notice—even to make!—
beauty, & God will say, what?
& God will say, who
the fuck are you, & what
the fuck is beauty, & how
dare you address Me, & what
the fuck is beauty, & what
have you, My nobody,
My terrible impulse, done

Jordan Escobar

Pack Animals

They say you have to have a bluegrass state of mind
to effectively wield molasses. And you have to run
over shifting landscapes, in gathered pulses, before
you know that sorghum swaying on the horizon
is just another way of saying good evening
to this day's toil. But you want more than speed
and more than strength. You want flavor. You want love.
You want someone to run their delicate fingers
down your back, to collect the sweat as drops of dew,
the early-starred sky building a dark wash
like flecks of paint splashed across a sorrel coat. At the end
of every day, you want to lie down in the merciful shade,
your sides bellowing, and have someone, anyone,
know the distances your body can carry.

Coby-Dillon English

The Fox Skull Trio

The boy dreamed himself a fox and he was running through the woods. Behind him were the sounds of angry voices, stomping feet, and the roar of torches; in front of him was the shadow of his own animal body, made large against the forest floor. The fox knew he was being chased, and he knew the people who were hunting him. He knew them by the sound of their feet on the earth. He knew them by the way they had chased away other wild things. He knew the only way to escape the woods is to run. The only way to escape the dream is to wake up.

The boy dreamed himself a fox or he dreamed the whole world was a fox, curled up in its sleep, with its snout tucked into its center. The People lived on its back among its red, bristly hairs that were actually trees grown in straight lines. The People didn't know that they lived on a fox-who-was-the-whole-world, and they still hunted the fox-boy. The People knew what dreaming could do. The fox-boy ran all over the fox-world's back, trying to find the center of the world. If he could lead the People down into the center, the fox-who-was-the-whole-world would open its jaws that were the size of mountains and swallow the People in one clean snap. As the fox-boy ran, he stomped his paws hard against the ground, hoping the world would wake up, that the fox-who-was-the-whole-world would save the boy. The boy knew that the world would save him because they were the same animal. The boy and the world were always the same.

The fox dreamed himself a boy with ten pink fingers and ten brown toes. He ran through the woods behind his grandparents' house on two legs behind his older brother. The trees in these woods were thin and tall with very few branches below the canopy. They were planted in lines like crops, and running between them was like moving through a kaleidoscope of corridors. Each step forward showed the boy another clean passageway he could run down, countless hallways that led to no rooms, just more lines. His brother ran ahead, bounded between the trees, switching lanes and directions erratically, laughing from just the act of moving, from just the joy of going from here to there. The boy laughed, too, but was afraid he would lose his brother. The gap stretched farther and farther between them, but as far apart as they became, they were never out of sight of each other. There was nowhere to hide in the parallel woods; everything was always straight ahead. The boy and his brother were together again when they came across a set of train tracks that cut through the trees. They stepped onto the tracks, turned their heads to look down both directions, and saw nothing but clean lines. They walked down the tracks, heel to toe, balancing on the two raised beams, holding hands over the middle. The boy stopped when he saw a small skull resting in front of his feet on his side of the tracks. His brother stopped, too, and the pair stared for a while. There wasn't a speck of flesh or fur left on the skull. Besides the fact that it was missing its bottom jaw, it was pristine. Every tooth was perfectly intact. The boy thought maybe it wasn't even real. Sitting there on the raised beam of the train tracks, the skull looked like it had been left there for them. The boy's brother said it must be a fox skull because of how small it was, just barely bigger than the size of the boy's fist with two large, sharp teeth towards the front. The boy had never seen a skull before, or even a real bone that hadn't belonged to a cooked chicken or turkey, and was surprised to see that it wasn't perfectly white like he had thought. This skull was more of a cream color, slightly warm in tone, soft even. He reached out to pick it up, ignoring his older brother's protests about germs and dead things. Holding the skull in his hands, the boy knew that it was a real skull, that it was so much its true self that it had merely seemed inauthentic. It was dense in his hands. He traced his thumb down from the peak of the head to the jagged opening at the end of the snout. The boy lifted the skull up so that he was looking into the place where the fox's eyes had been. The boy knew the fox was a predator. The eyes may face forward, and the teeth may be sharp, but look at how small this deadly skull was. The boy thought, *I have one of these inside of me. Not just a skull, but a fox skull. No one knows I am also a fox.* The boy carried the skull back to his grandparents' house, showed everyone there, let them look at the cream fox skull with their milky people eyes. His mother was mortified. His father said the boy could keep it. The fox never woke from the dream.

Austin Sanchez-Moran

Devouring an Angel

A small, white-winged angel arrives at a man slowly dying in a fallow wheat field. The man needs water. Instead of helping him, the high-toned angel begins imparting the meaning of life to the man. The angel says that angels come to those who are dying and deserve to know. The angel then makes a beautifully crafted Danish mid-century modern chair materialize. The man is confused and thirsty. The angel gives the man an ultimatum: Sit in the chair and relax or stand back and admire the craftsmanship of the chair. It is the only important decision that the dying man has to make in order to get into heaven.

While the angel is explaining all of this, the man has crawled closer to the angel. The man is in reach and has other plans. He lunges at the angel, grabbing its hairless leg. The angel struggles like an albatross in a fishing net. It screams and squawks. Then the man grabs ahold of its terribly flapping wings. Finally, holding the back of the angel's head, he slams its forehead into the hard ground, killing it. The man eats the parts of the angel he could stomach. He survives. Later, when he dies as an old man, there is no one there to direct him towards heaven or hell.

Dustin M. Hoffman

Bartleby's Resume

Bartleby
Scrivener
New York, NY

Objective

To be. To stay. But I'd prefer not to say why, and where is not important. Any corner where two walls meet, I can whittle away the hours of this life. Any room will do, really. One need not prefer one way or the other. But I prefer to prefer not to.

Skills

★ I'd prefer not to write copy. Though my spelling is impeccable, my handwriting clean as a letterpress, fast as a Gutenberg. Never has my pen's nib spilled a rogue ink spot. Your rushed words neaten through my steady hand. But does not the blank blotter paper carry more perfection? An unmarked page—unsullied by language, clean as a breath untaken—cannot be matched.

★ I'd prefer not to scrive, for the dim lighting obscures my vision. I'd prefer not to work by oil lamp, but the only natural light strains through the window faced by the neighboring office's brick wall. I've studied the mortar, its pale maze. I know every brick, each pore and crack in the clay exhumed from earth and baked in fire. Can you say you know your own child's face so well?

★ I'd prefer not to proof my own work or yours or Nippers' or Ginger Nut's or Turkey's. Let the original mistake be the final one. *Stet* and *stet* to world without end. Amen.

- ★ I'd prefer not to expedite mail delivery, replace office supplies, deliver case copy, and all other such menial tasks essential to a thriving office. I could, of course, perform each need with adroitness. But that has never been the issue. Preference persists.
- ★ I'd prefer not to place my finger at the crossing of the red string so that you may complete your knot—the knot binding this deed's paperwork, this land repossessed by the bank from Widow Skoglund, purchased by her husband from the United States government who claimed it from the Lenape people who borrowed it from God, if there ever was one to exist.

Scrivener 1843-1844, Lower Manhattan, New York

- ★ Copied legal documents, until I preferred not to. If you allow your eyes to connect like wires to your arms and hands, stretching that dim electric pulse all the way to fingertips, you might manage to work for eight hours without once needing to think. At first, it can be soothing as staring at brick.
- ★ Perpetually punctual. Always arrived early, for I preferred not to commute. I preferred never bother with leaving.
- ★ Enacted perfect record of honesty. Never once did I lie, and why perjure when one can abdicate every responsibility?
- ★ Maintained a neatly organized desk. Undisturbed. Untouched pens. Unmolested stack of copy. All as neat as virgin blotter paper.
- ★ Fostered collegial relationship with colleagues through the same method as desk organization. If no one speaks, no relationship might sour. Remember, it was Turkey who wanted to punch me. It was Ginger Nut who offered the cakes, who begged me eat anything. My placid demeanor painted pain across his expression, so that I preferred not to disturb him further. I placed a penny in his palm and accepted his mercy.
- ★ And I observed Martha, the cleaning woman who domesticated our building and swept up all those cake crumbs each night, scrubbed Turkey's tipsy ink spatters. When she found me curled on the wooden floor, staring into the corner, she brought me a quilt stitched with purple and blue diamonds. Eventually, she offered dinner. Eventually, she offered that I

might sleep in her bed through the hours when she cleaned. But undisturbed is best. Always best.
- ★ Exuded a "cadaverous" disposition.

Dead Letter Office 1840-1843, Washington, D.C.
- ★ Had no desk to manage, but my sorting table remained pristine.
- ★ Tended furnace, never allowing the coals to dull, three years of constant embers burning deep as sunset's glower. Bright until the night our office closed.
- ★ Created organizational systems to optimize efficiency. First, it was predictably alphabetical, piteous names drawn from the return labels, those who'd never learn they remained unheard. Later, we shifted to using addressed names, those lost ghosts. Later still, postage dates proved for faster sorting. Then organized by size and shape. Finally, devised a system of clutching letter to chest, closing eyes, scrying each letter's intent. From this information, I catalogued by emotion. But our system mattered little. Expedience toward the fire drove all.
- ★ Apprenticed under Charles Cronenworth, senior Dead Letter Office administrator. Charles never spoke, for he was mute. We communicated through a system of knuckle raps reverberating through the oaken table. If not at table, then kicks to shin and rump. Elegant silence professionalized our discourse.
- ★ Protected senders' privacy and honored lost recipients. Popular speculation assumes we collected valuables: currency, gold dust, unrequited engagement rings, locks of hair. On the contrary, we saved nothing. Even when we felt the bulge of relic stowed into the envelope's corner, we relinquished those talismans to the flame. No sign remained save for the furnace's crackle.

Gary Fincke

IQ Test

My mother said she had seen a photograph of a child prodigy's parents posed beside him as part of the good news feature of the seven o'clock news. "He's only twelve," she said, "and he's entering medical school and puberty at the same time; isn't that something? By the time he's your age, he'll be a surgeon, somebody able to have my life in his hands."

My mother loved stories about boy geniuses. Since I'd started first grade, my future was supposed to wear scrubs, wash its hands in scalding water, and answer a body's questions with skillfully handled blades, but I was already nineteen, too old for any description with the prefix "boy." For a while, as she went on about the child-doctor, I watched her preparing tomatoes for canning. Then, she asked the question she'd been holding inside all summer. "How's my doctor coming along?"

Steam rose toward the kitchen ceiling like expectations. When I didn't answer right away, she said she'd heard somewhere that the brightest people have the earliest memories. "I bet that boy remembers wearing diapers," she said. "What do you remember?"

That was a question I knew the answer to. "My head being shaved because of the ringworm you said I caught at the barbershop. Then everybody calling me 'baldy.'"

"That's when you were four," my mother said, sounding disappointed. "How about something from when you were three?"

I decided to go with something else from when I was four that must have happened earlier. "The day I started wearing those steel-braced shoes because I walked funny."

"See?" she said. "You were three years and seven months to the day. By then, everybody knew you were smart." She looked at the clock that hung on the wall above the kitchen sink as if she were about to announce the exact minute those braces had been set in place, but then she turned and sighed so heavily I knew what was behind all this were my recent grades. "They're less than perfect," was how she had put it when they'd arrived. As if she was uneasy mentioning the letter C or, I was sure, not daring to say D aloud because it was blasphemy. "Try to remember your toddler year," she finally said. Which I took for the pre-brace year, and what I remembered was nothing whatsoever, as empty of answers as I'd been for the final exam in organic chemistry.

"The super snow drifts," I said, beginning with something safe while my mother leaned back into those tomatoes, taking a stab at the winter of '77 when we still lived near Buffalo. I'd heard about that blizzard every late January when the anniversary of "the big one" rolled around. "There was one so high somebody stood on it and touched a live wire."

My mother started humming, and I coasted into the summer before. "Dad, in the new, used GTO, singing 'Afternoon Delight' while we drove to Niagara Falls."

"Yes!" my mother nearly screamed. "Yes, he about ruined that trip with all that talk about 'skyrockets in flight.'"

"And Barry Manilow," I said, figuring there must have been a hit that summer for my mother's favorite singer.

"'I Write the Songs,'" she said, and sang a few lines. "That's my boy," she said. "That's my brain surgeon coming back to life."

I kept on spellbinding her with my high IQ of nostalgia, but I didn't say a word about having already changed my major from pre-med to history. I loved following all those timelines that detailed how everything and everywhere and everybody became the way we were. If my mother asked when she finally found out, I'd start by saying they were like arteries and veins and capillaries, an enormous circulatory system.

I boarded the express trance through my year number one and rode it all the way back to my birth. I'd seen enough photographs to describe my mother's hair, how it was curled, held tight to her scalp with pastel pins. I knew the nurse would be saying, "It's a boy," that mystery still solved on the spot in 1974. I felt the doctor's gloved hands on my emerging head, heard the nurse saying, "One last push," giving that first day everything it needed to certify me as absolutely brilliant until, seeing her beaming beside a winter's worth of tomatoes in perfectly sealed jars, I vanished myself back into the sea of darkness inside her, sucking my thumb and kicking, then passing beyond gender and the wiring up of the brain, whatever insisted my genius was true, until I became just words my mother murmured to my father as he touched her or said to herself before she even knew him.

Michael Hardin

Washington Park, Anacortes

Three days after Christmas, my mother suggests we take a walk by the Pacific. It's fifty degrees with the first glimpse of blue sky in the five days we've been on Whidbey Island. I know she can't make a mile, much less three—she has neuropathy in her feet from diabetes. She tells me that she and my father will drive the loop in their truck.

My wife and children are eager for exercise. I need to get out of my parents' house. Our relationship works because I only talk to my mother every four months or so, and see them maybe once a year, although because of COVID it's been three.

The park is wooded, towering trunks covered in green. Julian, my fifteen-year old son, tries to determine north by the moss on the lodgepole pines. I learned that, too, in Royal Rangers, our church's scout group, but because of the years of Christian indoctrination and sexual abuse, I discount everything they said.

We stop at a large pine that has grown horizontally over the ocean, mere feet above the water. Blake, my twenty-year old daughter, proceeds out on it. She's intrepid and I haven't outgrown the fear she'll fall and I'll have to rescue her. She's safe, though—years of lessons and swim team have made her a stronger swimmer than me.

My parents have parked along the road. My mother stands at the edge telling my kids she climbed on this same tree with her four sisters when she was their age, visiting her grandparents. I try to picture my mother young and free to climb. I remember a vacation in Yosemite when I was six, and we inadvertently rode our bikes on a mountainous burro trail. My mother had my year-old brother on the back of her three-speed as my father led the way. They seemed immortal then.

My parents drive on ahead as my family continues the loop, stopping each time a side trail winds down to the ocean. My wife,

Claire, collects smooth stones, moss and seaweed, nature she can take back to Pennsylvania in her suitcase, organize in a glass bowl and display in her office.

The road leaves the sea and climbs the mountain. Blake and Julian, ten yards ahead, leap in unison as my wife takes a picture. At an overlook, I find myself positioned between my family and my parents: son, father, husband, each its own identity. My parents appear frailer than I remember when we visited before the pandemic. My children exhibit more independence, need me less each year. My wife struggles with anxiety; she relies on me at night to talk her down from the demons of her day.

I'm relieved my mother is not walking. Her disease is genetic, and I've worried for decades it'd strike me, too. At a visit a month ago, my doctor informed me based on a glucose test, I'm prediabetic. Cut back on the sugar and carbs, exercise fifteen minutes a day, and I should be fine. I don't tell my mother. I don't tell my children, either, but I'll have to—it's something they might inherit from me.

Today's hike is the first exercise I've gotten this trip. There's an arc of rainbow over the ocean—once a promise from God not to destroy us, now a picture taken with my phone I text to my friend.

Michael Hardin

Free Piano

Do you want a piano? I have one I could give you, a Kroeger upright grand, built in 1896. My grandfather's great-uncle, Henry, carved the bench by hand, inlaying a starburst in rare wood on the seat. I don't want to give it away; it's my inheritance from my grandparents, my only inheritance besides my name. I want to pass this piano down to my children, either my daughter or son, but it's big and weighs at least five hundred pounds. My daughter played it for six years, took lessons but never practiced much. And she tried to teach her brother, putting masking tape on the ivory keys with the names of the notes.

No one has played it in five years, not since we moved to our new house. It took a crew of four men and cost three hundred dollars to transport two miles. If you want the piano, you'll have to move it.

I remember my grandmother warning my siblings and me, "All liars shall have their part in the Lake of Fire," and playing Pentecostal hymns while she babysat us, back when we all lived in Southern California. That's all she ever played. *Make a joyful noise unto the Lord, all ye lands*. My family interpreted this verse as a commandment to make music. I learned the clarinet, played well enough by sixth grade to be part of our church's orchestra. It was a small church: a piano and organ, my father on trumpet along with another deacon, two violins and a baritone sax. I worried my clarinet would squeak, draw attention to me, and probably qualify as a sin, so mostly I just fingered my instrument with the orchestra during the song service and offertory. No one noticed.

I had married and moved to Pennsylvania when my grandmother died, and three years later my grandfather passed. They never owned much. As a child, I'd coveted the carved masks and elephants from their missionary trips to Africa and Asia, but those were taken by my aunt when she assumed the leadership of United Evangelical Churches, my grandfather's mission organization. The piano and a treadle sewing machine: the only things left in their house when my father went out after the funeral. My sister inherited the sewing machine even though she played piano for ten years. I felt like I needed a tangible reminder of my grandparents, so I asked for the piano.

The piano sits in our library, surrounded by five bookshelves. I should also tell you, it's out of tune. It hasn't been serviced since before my father drove it out to Pennsylvania in the back of his pickup truck, maybe fourteen years by now.

I've read that no one wants old pianos anymore. People just take them to the dump and get rid of them. I don't want to do that, but what happens when my wife and I move back to California and retire in a small apartment? If neither child wants a massive piano from great-grandparents they never met, then what do I have to pass down besides my name? Do we really need objects to remind ourselves of the dead?

Can a poem have the same weight as a wooden instrument on which they create their own music? I write for and about them, without the burden of Christianity. Poems will be their inheritance, a book more personal than a piano. Maybe heirlooms should stay in the past. My mother-in-law has a house full of antiques that have been in her family for generations, and my wife is an only child. My kids will inherit Minton and Fostoria from her side of the family, as well as furniture, but they don't seem particularly interested in those, either.

Are you sure you don't want a piano? I'll even help you move it if you have a truck.

Michael Hardin

Burying My Grandfather

My mom's voice on the answering machine told me my grandfather had died. My dad's father. The message mentioned the date of the funeral, a date that had already passed. We had been in Salt Lake City for a week visiting my wife's mom and aunt. My daughter, six, and my son, one, had never met their great-grandfather. A legacy I chose to keep from them.

The funeral was in Evansville, an eleven-hour drive I could have made, like I did when my grandmother died three years before, the last time I saw him. My wife had her cell phone; my parents knew her number.

I don't believe in God or heaven, or even a soul. Maybe that's why saying goodbye to him was so important, or maybe I just needed a ritual of closure.

When I was young, he lived across the street in Monrovia. I visited him in his office at United Evangelical Churches. He let me take the stamps off letters from around the world. He gave me the leftover coins from his missionary trips to Africa and Asia. I picked weeds and collected pecans in his backyard. We also dug through the park trash bins for pop bottles and aluminum cans to take to the recycler.

When I was ten, he took me and my siblings to Kentucky to visit our relations, living and dead. He preached a revival meeting while we were there, called forth the sick and demon-possessed and anointed them with oil. He touched one woman on the forehead and she collapsed on the floor. I witnessed this from the front row, next to my grandmother. He could no longer be just my grandpa.

My grandparents moved their ministry to Georgia, and I, too, left LA and the church. Twenty years later, they attended my wedding, visibly older, my grandmother confined to a wheelchair by a series of strokes, my grandfather reduced to caregiver, but still wielding his Bible, his ecclesiastic collar and cross. I would not see my grandmother alive again.

I was in Pennsylvania and my grandfather underground in Indiana. Across from our two-hundred-year-old farmhouse was a wetlands, fed by Sechler Run. I often went down to the creek to contemplate. This time I took a shovel.

Beneath a rotting sugar maple, I dug a hole, big enough for my grandfather. I planned to make it six feet deep but hit rock after eighteen inches. It'd have to do. I made a figure of a man out of discarded bricks and found an empty soda can for his spirit. I found another can for my other grandfather, the one who predicted the Rapture three times in the 1980s and then died of prostate cancer. A third can, for the scout leader from my church who sexually abused me and died of a heart attack before I could kill him. I even found a can for my father, still alive. I threw them all in and filled the hole. I sat there for an hour or two, cried a little, unsure what any of it had meant.

Stephen Lackaye

The Beast Is Dead and We Have Built a City in Its Ribs

So long we dreamed its hunger and it stood
for angers we lagged centuries to name.
The clamor in its mange shook from the shanks
of brick through rooms that had inured us
to sequester, every shadow fell exhausted,
all our weather turned to teated sky and slaver.
I used to shave and listen to the early workers
walk the spine of the abandoned railway
closed by prehistoric fire, singing of the glory
of the skyline and the fullness of our bread.
Now, the beast is dead, and we have built
a city in its ribs. We've wrenched the nails out
of the windows, cleared the calls for help
from bills, let the talons keep the names
of the bridges they replaced. Assured of honest
work, we shape the city back into itself
before the beast was heard, but not before
we built the city in the image of its ribs.
The beast is dead, and the ombudsmen spend
the budget surplus on new dress robes.
Black-clad recruiters find their favored corners;
the failed shipyard's still our top employer.
Hummingbirds, like pine cones, litter the grounds
of private gardens, and everywhere young girls
are caught in the act of domesticating jaguars.
You can practically hear the harbingers
humming in their torpor. If you listen more closely,

the dream persists to walk tomorrow's man
to the upset of the river, his plea suppressed
in the pelt from factory to crown of bridge,
the coin of moon lost in the clutch of the ribs,
upstream of the policemen's tireless dredging.

Maureen Clark

Ten Coins

I.

At the entrance to an eighth-century Anglo-Saxon longhouse
archeologists find the ghosts of post holes
and an offering of animal skulls and flint blades

II.

Cadaver dogs can smell a human body
that has been dead for 200 years Yesterday police found the bodies
of those two kids from Idaho missing for nine months
buried in their stepfather's backyard

III.

Thirty feet below street level in New York City a slave graveyard
of 15,000 skeletons discovered Hard to believe
you could lose a whole cemetery but then
where do you put something you don't want to remember

IV.

Something you should know
if you are digging for Roman coins in Britain ten is a hoard
and must be reported to the authorities

V.

On a cliff   overlooking the North Sea   a twelfth-century church
and on the doorstep   a mound of infant bones
that no one understands

VI.

Of the one hundred and fifteen slaves   buried in the graveyard
at Monticello   half were children   their bones
already misshapen   from hard work   and malnutrition

VII.

What if your last chance   is a dog's nose
trained to remove layers of smells   to hit the mark
the decomposing body   air shaken with old blood   rotting flesh
that sets the dogs to barking

VIII.

The coin you find   must be cleaned   and dated by an expert
use the tip of your trowel   to lift it from the dirt
Handle it with delicate fingers

IX.

Remember that girl   shot by her husband
then rolled up in a mattress   taken to the dump
They let the dogs loose   but it took a long time
Her white cheeks   were an unbelievable odor
coming into bloom   when the dogs finally found her
growing rank   among the garbage

X.

Ten coins hardly seem like a hoard   but whoever buried it
wanted to be   the only one   who could dig it up

Mary Simmons

Little Red

I wash bloodstains from the tub
with cold water and lemon soap.
What I wanted: teeth enough
to scatter the dark, a snout trained
on lies. To flick breathless
through the pines. A moon to swallow
off the lake, dripping light
down my chin. Thimblefuls of death.
What I received: a body.

Lynn Domina

Theft

Liz says the trick is to let your heart beat fast while your hands stay steady slipping the Snickers or razor blades or hair ties into your pocket.

At one time or another, I've thought about stealing money from a bank, money from a cash register, an icon of St. Mary Magdalene, a glittery postcard of the Golden Gate Bridge, and someone's baby.

Huckleberry Finn says Pap told him it ain't stealing if you mean to pay it back.

Josh says catching a glimpse of your neighbor's hand after he's asked for three cards might be dangerous, but it isn't stealing.

Jesus says the thought is as good as the deed.

Xavier says he can't forgive himself for stealing his grandmother's TV when he was high.

The list price of *Steal This Book* is $18.99.

Andre says the government will steal the shirt off your back before it'll give the little guy a break.

Mark sounds like a hyena when he denies guilt. Noël says no like she's singing. I'd asked them if they'd ever opened my desk drawers when I was away. I'd asked them if they'd seen my envelope of foreign currency, my euro notes with their Romanesque doorways, my Canadian loonies, my rupees to remind me that I can always touch Gandhi.

Keith says we take things too far. Pretty soon, he says, we'll call baiting a hook theft from the robin.

When someone says you took the words right out of my mouth, it's not an accusation. When someone says you took me for a fool, it is.

Othello says a man's not robbed if he doesn't know it.

What about the worm? Or the fish?

Michael says private property is theft. Always? I ask. Always, he says.

Jessica says rape was once classified under theft, not from the woman but from her husband or father. She says her state's penal code devotes 363 paragraphs to theft, addressing all manner of property, from illegal stills to prescription pads to a landowner's rightful share of the harvest.

Is importing cotton in order to export clothing to those who've picked the cotton theft? What about throwing a man off a train when he's paid for his ticket?

The law says a master cannot steal from a slave because a slave, being property, cannot own property.

Heather warns us not to mistake land acknowledgments, *This conference occurs on the traditional homeland of the Anishinabe people*, as reparation for theft.

Logic permits what ethics excludes and vice versa.

When someone says no like a song, they're lying.

Every time.

Matt Barrett

Thief

Every day, a man tries to break into my house. He knows I'm there, but it doesn't stop him. Through the window, I'll scold him when he cuts one of my screens. And I'll call his name from the other side of my door when he starts to unfasten the locks. He's gotten in a handful of times, usually when I let my dog outside. I'll find him in my kitchen, taking a few things from the pantry before scurrying back to his house. He lives with his wife and two kids in a beautiful home at the end of the street. At night, he comes over to apologize. He changes in the daytime, he says. When his wife's at work and his children go to school. He can't help himself—the man who enters my house isn't even really him. I say I've heard that story before, and he looks off, embarrassed, and thanks me for not hurting him when he snuck in through the garage.

A friend of mine says to report him. That the man has everything—a family, a house, a nice big yard, and two sleek cars. What could he want from you? My friend looks at my house, the single bathroom, the Tupperware left in the sink. A picture of a girl I used to know.

I mean, if it were the other way around, I'd understand, he says.

When the man comes back, I threaten to call someone. But he knows I won't. I wouldn't know how to explain it to his family. Or to him, after all these times he's thanked me.

I think about moving, but I'm not sure where I'd go. I think about going back to work, but I'm afraid of what I'd come home to. I think maybe I should just get rid of all this stuff, but I doubt that's what he's after.

When I'm out of ideas, the man offers me one. Get a parrot, he says. He's scared of birds, always has been. Especially the ones that talk.

I buy a macaw, train it to say a few phrases. Like get lost, go away, and run.

In a few weeks, the man works up the nerve to come in, despite the parrot inside. It escapes through the door he enters, landing in the silver maple behind my house. It perches there for days. I call its name, but it doesn't come. I leave its food out by the back door. After a week, I remove my screens, throw open the windows and doors so it knows to come inside.

I sit there and wait, ignoring the man who enters and exits freely. The parrot watches me from its branch. At some point, it has to eat something. At some point, it has to fly. As the summer ends, I shout for it to go south. It calls back: Go away! I say, It won't be warm enough for you. It shouts back: Run!

The parrot's food and cage go missing. It has no reason to come inside. I close the windows, shut the doors. Leaves fall in yellow and reds. Blue sits on its branches. One night, the man comes over. We shine a spotlight on the tree.

The man's brought beers from his house, and milk chocolates, wrapped in golden foil.

He says, I wonder why it won't just fly.

The man passes me one of the chocolates. He hands me a second beer.

I mean, it got up there, didn't it? It must be able to fly.

I say, It must.

Then why isn't it flying?

I shake my head. I explain I don't have answers.

The man looks over at me. He clinks his glass with mine. Hey, he says. We're friends, don't you think? I mean, most of the time, we're friends.

He sits beside me on a bench by the kitchen windows.

He grabs a bag of chips from my pantry closet, opens it over the counter.

Chip? he asks. He holds the bag toward me. I take a handful, he eats a few.

Damn shame it won't just fly.

Keith J. Powell

Mysterious Teeth

My dentist discovered wreckage from a Lockheed Model 10-E Electra lodged between my maxillary second and third molars. He didn't need to tell me what it meant.

"It's hers," I said. "Amelia Earhart's plane."

He tapped the backlit X-ray of my jaw with his green Sharpie. "We just won't know for sure until we get in there and investigate," he said. "Let's schedule an appointment for tomorrow morning."

I called my insurance company from the parking lot. A sour agent advised me the procedure would only be covered if the slippery scraps of metal excavated were found to have significant historical or cultural value. I advised *her* that uncovering the final fate of one of aviation's great pioneers would have significant historical and cultural value to spare, and hung up.

At home, I streamed old episodes of *Unsolved Mysteries*, and let Robert Stack's gravelly promise that I could help solve a mystery soothe my turbulent hopes and stubborn doubts. After eighty years of wonder, we were *so* close.

When I arrived the next morning, my dentist's usually tidy waiting room was crammed with fedoraed paparazzi. Flashbulbs popped and sizzled while I updated my emergency contact, and did my best to ignore their snickering questions about the vintage aviator's scarf and goggles I'd worn to commemorate this momentous day. The cacophony teased my stomach into barrel rolls, and I wondered if this was how Amelia felt every time she climbed into the cockpit to shatter some fantastic unknown. Finally, a hygienist appeared in the doorway and saved me, ushering me back into the operatory.

Seated and bibbed in the small, hushed space, I discovered a poster tacked to the ceiling. *Everything I Need to Know About Life I Learned in Preschool.* I considered its counsel to *Listen with my heart* as my dentist meticulously arranged instruments in perfect equidistance across a paper-lined tray. Just before 10 a.m., he tugged on a clean pair of blue gloves and reached for the gas. I stayed his hand.

"No," I said.

He plucked a steel shepherd's hook from his tray and twirled it between latexed fingers like a tiny, wicked dancer.

"In cases like these, I really recommend putting patients under," he said. "It's going to hurt. There's significant rot along the gumlines."

"I need to be awake for this," I said. "I can take the pain. What I can't take is the not knowing."

Will Musgrove

No Pickles

Didn't I say no pickles? I thought after noticing one sticking out from underneath the bun of my cheeseburger. I hate pickles. Can't stand the taste or texture. Not wanting to make a fuss, though, I kept driving and decided to remove the pickle myself. I lifted the bun, and a glinting light briefly blinded me. Rubbing my eyes and blinking, I saw it, a tiny window nestled in the middle of the beef patty. I peered through the window, one eye closed, and there I was, maybe five or six, scarfing a Happy Meal in my dad's old station wagon. Good times.

I tapped on the windowpane like a kid tapping the side of an aquarium, and my younger self glanced up before returning to his french fries. That was OK. I was happy just seeing him happy.

When I got back to my apartment, my girlfriend Jackie asked why I wasn't eating. I considered showing her the window but decided against it, decided to hoard it for myself. Instead, we got into the same old fight about how I was keeping something from her, and she stormed out, shouting we were through. I thought about chasing after her, but the comfort of the window pulled at me. Alone, I looked through it again and saw our first date, saw us walking along the river and talking about how this—good view, good company—was enough, and it was like we'd never broken up.

With a fingernail, I pried the window open a smidge. In the process, though, the beef around the window gave way a little, so I stopped, scared I'd lose all I had left of her. I stopped, pressed my lips to the small crack, and whispered, "I love you." She gazed across the river and then reached down and grabbed my younger self's hand as if she'd heard me.

The next morning, I convinced myself it was all a strange fever dream and got ready for work. On my way out, I spotted the cheeseburger on the kitchen counter. I told myself there was no window, just a pickle. But when I lifted the bun, there it was. I knew I should have called Jackie then and told her what I'd found, should have asked for forgiveness. Or at least I should have been on my way to the office. I knew I shouldn't look, but I did anyway because life is hard and it's easier to just look. I looked and saw high school summer vacation, saw my buddies and me scooping the loop, saw having time to drive in circles.

I called in sick and pretended to have food poisoning. Sinking into my sofa, I looked through the window to watch the happiest moments of my life play back like home movies. I looked and looked. Each viewing was full of calorie-rich nostalgia. Days zoomed by. Months. Years, maybe. Soon, the window was in reruns. I'd watched my first kiss a few dozen times, watched myself hit my lone Little League home run again and again. I watched these memories so much it started to feel like they didn't even belong to me, like I was really watching the cheeseburger's life play back, not mine.

There was nothing fresh to see, so the cheeseburger started to rot. Mold grew on the bun. The beef patty was turning gray. A sepia tone coated everything like butter. And I missed Jackie. Even now, as I prepare to look through the window one last time, prepare to smash the window with a pebble, I think about her, but it's too late. That's why I'm hoping to see my idling vehicle in that drive-thru, hoping I'll be able to tell my past self, "Remember, no pickles, please. No pickles."

Kevin Sterne

There's Nothing Tall in Illinois

That spruce in Frankfort. That obelisk of timber like a NASA rocket. That Cousin Itt dressed in blue singing dull aqua. No leaves—just needles that won't cut you, needles just pining old blue. Tallest on the block. Tallest until it fell in the '94 tornado. Grandma watched it out the kitchen window. Shaking, bending, almost breaking until it did. Whipping in the wind like witches in winter. The sky was purple and the sun was gray and the birds hid in the window wells lest dead in the drain ditches. They say the tallest tree gave in because it had more to give. The royal we is a silent we on a payphone. Calling home. Calling Grandma in the basement calling Grandpa at the bar. That summer he trimmed that tree because it poked the house. Gave it some shape and upset Grandma all at once. She stayed silent four days and turned on the TV she never watched. The home shopping channel sold over-ear headphones, plastic bags to cook a turkey, a chair to align the back. She bought it all to spite him. They brought you over, all five years of you, because a child can ease tensions. You kissed Grandma on the lips because you didn't know what a grandma kiss was. She had onion soup for lunch. Tornado touched down on Plainfield High School, ripped it apart like paper torn. Two towns over, eight traffic lights, two Dunkin Donuts, nine banks, the old Les Brothers in front of the Kmart. Water treatment plant. Small towns only small to the uninitiated. Nine times ten plus four. In the middle of it all, a construction crew moved a boulder by truck bed across the county. Remnant of the Wisconsin glacier, as big as two bodies curled around each other belly to belly, hip bone to blood and blood to dirt. In the middle of it all the Caterpillar truck driven by a boy barely a man with baseball aspirations and practical needs suited for a job driving trucks or digging holes at the cemetery between games of independent ball, third base with ghost-runner rules, day cash meal money. Slapped a plaque on the rock and placed it at the entrance of a forest with a four-car parking lot. Named it after the French. Joliet. In the middle of it all the tallest spruce split from the roots and surrendered across the lawn. Tip touched the street. All the streets are named after trees. Hickory, ash, walnut. Chestnut, sycamore, larch. No spruce, though. They carved it up with a chainsaw and Grandma cried. They brought you over to ease sadness and you hugged her but gave no kiss. You played in the creek with grocery bags over your feet. They left the stump as memorial. Grandma died then Grandpa died. House sold. Chair garage-saled off. That ballplayer bought it for his slipped disc and later on he killed himself. Everyone's buried on the same row in Pleasant View Cemetery. You visit and stand before them and imagine a golden glow like love growing inside you, growing and filling you up, filling you up and spilling down your legs into the ground where it kisses the dead. You're a payphone. You're trying to understand that you'll never understand your place in all of this. You're writing everything down for your dementia days. In your head you swing a bat at everything you don't understand. Look out at a horizon that only ends with the curving Earth. Think about that tree. All the history seized in needles. All the rhymes ringing in the dead. Screws in holes with no end. Just turning and turning and tightening nothing. They rebuilt that school. They closed that Kmart. That ballplayer's still swinging that bat somewhere. That rock is still there.

Shreya Fadia

Team Spirit

It's 5:32 a.m., and Ally's already in the basement in her hot-pink-spangled Team Spirit-brand bike shorts and coordinating sports bra, her eyeshadow the yellow-green of new-sprung leaves. The look is decidedly a bold one—skintight, a pain to get into, leaving her middle-aged spread and too-thick thighs on full display. But Erica S. had sported the exact same combo during a recent Sunday Pre-Brunch Crunch, and, on a mission to follow her bliss and to blow past her comfort zones, Ally had decided to take the plunge after payday: it was "add to cart" to "shipping soon" and then onto her doorstep in no time at all.

At ten 'til the hour, she's done with her warm-up drills and dynamic stretches; she's ready to go. She clips into the pedals, checks her makeup in the still-dark screen of her Team Spirit monitor, and then, with a touch of her finger, powers the bike up. As she navigates from the home screen over to the live schedule and hits "join class," the pre-workout anticipation jitters up and down her spine. She glances up at the framed mantras she'd found in the clearance bin at work and keeps displayed on the wall before her—*You got this*, one of them says in orange sans serif script. *No complaints. No excuses,* says another in loopy millennial pink. *Yes, you can.*

"You *got* this," Ally says aloud to the empty basement. "*I* got this. *I* can."

Three minutes to go time, and she's second-guessing if it's really an all-out Alejandro day or if she's more in the mood for the chill vibes of a Danny Chin replay, maybe the one where he'd complimented her username—picked hers alone out of so many hundreds, actually shaped the syllables of it with that perfect mouth. Alejandro's playlists reliably get her heart rate up, and his witty banter helps to tick the minutes away, but there is just something about Danny Chin's cool and quiet charm, the way he looks into the camera—head tilted, hair mussed just so, attention unwavering, unflinching, unblinking, as if he can see her, all of her, peer deep into the heart of her—that Ally can't resist.

But too late, there he is: Alejandro Gutiérrez Delgado, streaming live to her screen, coiffed and shined and pressed and primped, his hundred-watt smile—impossibly bright, impossibly white—blindingly on.

"Hello hello hellooo, Spirit Fam," his voice calls over the pumping music. "How we all doing on this glorious Friday morning?" He waits a beat, beaming at the camera, unabashedly flirting with it, before continuing on. "We're coming at you live from our Chicago studio and, though it may be snowing out there, it's gonna get hot up in here real fast, and not just because we're all looking damn good. We're going to be *working* today. I hope you came *Ready. To. Sweat,*" he says, adopting a boxer's stance in his saddle, playfully jabbing at the camera, a one-two, one-two punch punctuating his last few words.

Upon hearing Alejandro's voice and seeing his tremendous presence fill her screen, lighting it up, Ally forgets all about her hesitation. How could she ever have doubted him? Nothing beats a live Alejandro class, and it isn't just the muscled expanse of him, his astonishing Adonis-like physique, his bulging biceps, the peaks and plunging valleys of his calves and quads—though that is undoubtedly a part of the appeal; she can't deny it. But there is so much more to him than looks; the attraction runs more than skin-deep. Rather, it is his aura, his energy, his 6:00 a.m. exuberance, his authenticity and sass, the says-exactly-the-right-thing-when-you-need-it-the-most-ness of him, how he just always *knows*; his positivity and his excitement contagious, pushing her past her limits to unimaginable heights.

"Let's get pedaling," Alejandro says, and as his legs surge, gazelle-like, effortless, into motion, he stretches out one arm to the camera, toward Ally, reaching, reaching, inviting her to join, to take his hand in her own.

Ally starts pedaling; her metrics start to climb, and already, even before she's really working, before the endorphins have kicked in, she feels something like joy crescendoing up. There, in her basement, it's just the two of them, in it together, locked in for the whole ride, from warm-up to cool-down, an entire journey before sunrise, Ally and Alejandro, Alejandro and Ally, each revolution of their legs bringing them closer, traversing the same path toward something ineffable, inarticulable.

"Get on up out of those saddles, Spirit Animals. It's time."

The music rushes, the beat picks up, and Ally rises from her seat. She's breathless, but still she feels invincible, weightless, and as her pedals turn and turn, she takes flight.

At work that day, Ally keeps her head down and remains quiet, counting down the hours until she can leave, measuring them out in twenty-minute increments, mentally crossing them off one by one: Twenty-four Just-for-Fun class lengths. Down to twenty. Later, fifteen more to go.

This week, she's on holiday-display duty, tasked with replacing cardboard-cutout turkeys and horns of plenty, garlands of faux yellow and russet and orange leaves, with plastic boughs of holly, inflated snowmen, empty boxes wrapped in green and red and gold. She usually hates this time of year—the influx of disgruntled customers, the extra hours, the eggnog-scented candles, the manufactured holiday cheer, the achingly bitter Indiana cold, and, amid it all, her aloneness—but there's a spring in her step this season; she's suffused with lightness.

She attributes it all to her early-morning workouts; to the lower, however incremental, number on her scale; the newfound strength in her legs and heart; the sense of accomplishment and purpose she leaves the bike with after each journey, the profoundness of it all; the climbs and hills and transformations, the sweat and the tears and, yes, even the chafing she's endured over the past year; three to four—sometimes up to five—times a week, all before most people are even awake. But, the lion's share of her reinvention she owes to her instructors, her coaches, to Alejandro, to Danny Chin, to Maddie and Aditya, to Erica S., Erika H., and Erica R., even to Brock and Halima and Ilana; all of them are in it with her, in the fold of the Team Spirit family, *her* family. She's a better, more complete person for it all. Because of them, she has the strength to be present in her life, to withstand customers and coworkers, to show up for her mother.

Yes, you can, Ally tells herself when she realizes all the tinsel she spent hours wrapping around the aisle signs has fallen off.

You've done harder things, she reminds herself after a metal snowflake gashes a two-inch cut down her arm. *You got this.*

In the break room, where she sits alone eating her ham-and-cheese sandwich and her dessert of sliced apple, as she listens to her twenty-something-year-old coworkers discuss their Friday-night plans, or out on the floor, where couples and families peruse happily while pushing heavily laden carts, she remembers her morning ride: Alejandro's energy, the fist bumps she received from mom2monsters92 and smellsl1keteamsp1r1t and rydes4cronuts78 and nodramallama355, then afterward, peeling off her sweat-slick shorts, the hot pink darkened to near red, and that sense of fulfillment, the fullness in her chest; how radiant she felt in that moment, knowing that she was part of something, meant something, belonged.

I am worthy, she thinks. *I have found my purpose and my people. I am never alone.*

At four, Ally punches out, footsore, an ache in her lower back. Outside, the day is dull, the sky a lifeless gray, the air bracingly cold. She ducks her head as she walks into the wind, her green CostsLess employee vest bundled under her arm. An inch of icy snow films her car. With her sleeve, she brushes what she can reach from the roof and windshield and then sits with the engine idling to let the rest melt off.

While she waits, she pulls her phone out and navigates to the Team Spirit forums on SaidIt. She scrolls past best-ride round ups, questions about bike set-up, reports of technical glitches, the obligatory "why spin when you can ride a bike outside" post, until she finds the daily discussion thread. She skims through it to look for fresh gossip and has just about decided to close the tab when something catches her eye, a post from earlier that afternoon by a user named crypticmonkey123:

> *A little birdie told me that TS is beta-testing an all-new immersive user experience, like nothing anyone has ever seen before. Anyone have any details/know how to get on the list to try it out? Curious what this could be ....*

The post has been upvoted once and so far has only two responses, the first from someone named dogmomboo and a second from a user named sweatbloodnotears:

> *No idea but I'm stoked to find out. Consider me signed the f up lol*, says the first reply at 1:05.
>
> The second, at 3:42: *Whatever happened to delivering content users actually want rather than adding all these bells and whistles no one asked for? I swear, this company has really gone downhill—I mean, selling their bikes at CostsLess? Talk about lowest common denominator. They just keep catering to these lonely, pathetic AF, "diverse" users who jumped on the trend wagon and who actually buy the* you can do it *drivel the instructors keep shilling. And don't even get me started on that overpriced, tacky apparel line ....*

A thunk as a chunk of ice slides from Ally's roof to the windshield, and Ally puts her phone aside. She is flushed with shame, sudden and burning, but she'll miss visiting hours if she doesn't get going.

Ally fights back the tears, takes a few deep breaths, and tries to pull herself together. She turns on the wipers and watches their back-and-forth motion until they push the chunk of ice off the glass. With a clearer mind, she backs out of the parking spot.

"You belong. You are worthy," she says aloud as she heads toward the parking-lot exit. "Don't rent out your headspace to jerks. You don't need that negativity in your life."

You belong. You are worthy. Don't believe their lies, she repeats under her breath, over and over, for the rest of the drive, an incantation to keep her demons at bay.

A visit to her mother followed by a quarter of a pizza, a half a box of wine, and a comfort rewatch of several episodes of her favorite baking show—the one in which all the contestants are actually kind—help put the SaidIt posts out of Ally's mind. But the next morning brings it all tumbling back; when Ally powers on her Team Spirit bike, she's greeted with a pop-up message:

Congratulations! You are among an elite, exclusive group of members we are inviting to participate in a 30-day trial of a brand-new, one-of-a-kind, state-of-the-art Team Spirit user experience. Press OK to accept.

Ally skips over the fine print beneath the message to hover her finger over the green OK button, hesitating only momentarily before agreeing. What does she have to lose?

Her screen goes dark and then a blue download-status bar appears, beneath which, Ally is disappointed to see, is an estimated download time of an hour and fifty-four minutes. It is nearly quarter 'til the hour; she'll miss Erika H.'s live 9 a.m. Saturday HIITin' It Up class she's had on her schedule, but there's nothing for it now.

Ally heads upstairs to the cramped kitchen and puts on some coffee. On a whim while she waits, she pulls out her phone and navigates to yesterday's Team Spirit daily discussion thread on SaidIt to check for updates about the trial, but the original post and all the replies, of which there had apparently been a couple dozen, have been deleted, and at the end of the thread, there's a note from a moderator to keep things civil.

Ally quickly skims through the more recent posts but finds nothing of note. A search of the Team Spirit official website and social-media pages similarly turns up no leads. She sighs, pours herself some coffee, and settles in to wait out the remaining—she checks the time—now hour and forty-five minutes.

When Ally returns to the basement, the bike's monitor glows a cheerful blue-white; on the display screen, the download status bar is gone, and in its place is a new message: *Welcome to your one-of-a-kind Team Spirit user experience, personalized to better meet your individual needs. Press Next to continue onto A Path to a Different Tomorrow™, and you'll soon be on your way to a brand-new you.*

Ally climbs onto the bike, clips into her pedals, and then hits the green Next button, but to her dismay, the screen goes blank, dimming to gray-black, only her own frowning reflection staring back. She presses the bike's power button, holds it down, releases, tries it again, but all to no avail; the screen remains dark. She unclips from the pedals and climbs down from the saddle to check the power supply at the wall.

Ally has just begun to jostle the plug in its outlet when it happens: a sudden sound like glass shattering, followed by a blaze of white—blindingly, eye-wateringly, achingly bright—light. Ally squints in the glare, holding an arm up over her face to shield her eyes from it. And then, from somewhere deeper in the basement, from over near her mother's faux Christmas tree and boxed-up holiday decorations, a rustle, a voice. The blazing light dims, and Ally lowers her arm. A dark shape breaks away from the shadows and moves toward her.

"Hello, hello, hello," the voice says.

Ally knows that voice, knows it well—at this point, almost better than her own.

"It's a joy to meet you, bonanafanafofally," the voice says, and then, the dark shape steps out into the grayish light, and there he is, all six-feet-something-inches of him, impossibly tall, impossibly broad, impossibly *there*, flickering a little, once or twice, but then settling into clarity, the edges of him sharpening, inchoate no more.

At first, Ally doesn't believe what she's seeing. How could she? It just isn't possible. It can't be real. But the longer she stares at the figure, the harder it is to deny what's before her. It's him, undeniably so, or at least some version of him: Alejandro Gutiérrez Delgado, dressed in orange cycling shorts and a purple Team Spirit-branded muscle tee, walking toward her, toward *Ally*, right there in the basement of her mother's home.

"How are you on this fantabulous Saturday morning?"

Alejandro tilts his head to one side, studying Ally, who stares back, unable to look away, unable to do *anything*.

"How are you on this fantabulous Saturday morning, bonanafanafofally?" Alejandro asks again some moments of silent staring later, and then he tilts his head in the other direction.

He's waiting for her to answer, Ally realizes, and so she ventures a response. "Fi—I'm fine," she says.

Alejandro's expression brightens immediately. "Delighted to hear it! So, bonanafanafofally, are you ready to *Work ... It ... Out?*" he says.

Tentatively, Ally reaches a hand toward Alejandro's arm, but she stops with a few inches of space still remaining between them. Alejandro watches her hand's approach, but he doesn't pull back or otherwise respond, so Ally moves her hand an inch closer, then another, and another, until she's just a hairsbreadth away.

Ally knows he isn't really there. She knows that she is either hallucinating the whole thing or that he is just an exceptionally lifelike hologram constructed with light and lasers and mirrors and computer programming. She knows his solidity is an illusion and that the laws of physics and reality and logic make anything else an impossibility. She fully expects for her hand to pass through him, to find nothing there but the absence of him, proof that she needs to lay off the CostsLess boxed wine, never mind the employee discount.

But still, even so, even knowing all that, even expecting exactly what she finds, she is nevertheless surprised and, yes, disappointed—

beyond disappointed, shattered—when her hand passes right through Alejandro's arm, confirming that what she had suspected of his incorporeality is fact.

Alejandro's arm flickers where her hand passes through it. But then—and this, to Ally, seems important, signifies *something*, though she can't, in the moment, say exactly what—he doesn't disappear, doesn't otherwise change, doesn't come back different; he *stays*.

"So, bonanafanafofally, are you ready to work it out?" Alejandro repeats.

She nods, and Alejandro snaps his fingers, and as if by magic, a second bike appears next to Ally's. Alejandro climbs into his saddle and clips in his shoes, and Ally follows suit. Music blares from the speakers of Ally's bike, which has lit up and jumped to a new screen, in the center of which is only a button that says *START*.

"Let's do this, bonanafanafofally," Alejandro says.

Ally presses the button. She's ready to go.

Twenty days through the thirty-day trial and Ally has never felt more alive. Her life with Alejandro—the personalized one-on-one classes, an in-home coaching experience like no other—is so much more, so much better than the Team Spirit classes she'd hitherto taken, better than anything she could have asked or hoped for.

After that first class, once she'd ended her workout, gotten down from her bike, and turned it off, she'd assumed that Alejandro would disappear and probably for good. But when she'd powered the bike back on just a minute later—just to see what would happen, just to *know*—there he was again, this time with barely even a flicker, still in the same orange cycling shorts and purple muscle tee, sweatier than they'd been before, his hair ever so slightly disheveled.

"Back so soon, bonanafanafofally?" he'd said. "I love your commitment—I'm *here* for it—but we pushed hard today. Why not take some time to rest and recover? I think it will do you some good. I'd be happy to guide you through some stretches. Just say the word."

"I wanted to see if you'd come back. I wanted to see if you're real," she'd said.

He'd nodded sympathetically. "I understand. But I'm not going anywhere, bonanafanafofally. If you'd like, feel free to leave your bike powered on, and I'll stay right here, right where I am. If you say, 'Enable roaming mode,' I can even move around your home, up to a distance of fifteen feet from your bike, though our brilliant, tireless Team Spirit engineers are currently working to expand that range even as we speak."

They haven't spent a day apart since that.

Despite the brevity of the time they've had together, Alejandro has managed to become so much more than a coach: he's a roommate—no, a friend, a companion, a true constant in Ally's life. Sure, he still only knows her as bonanafanafofally, even though she tries, daily, to teach him her real name; and sure, he has only managed to make it as far as the basement door before he starts glitching horribly; and sure, he is basically a glorified virtual assistant, only hyper-focused on health and fitness; and yes, there is also the matter of his becoming confused at times and looping over and over again through a prerecorded error script and needing to be power-cycled if Ally leaves her bike on for too long. But so what? What does any of that matter? None of that changes the truth of what he is for her. None of it changes the fact that she is really on a path to a different tomorrow, that she's becoming—no, she already *is*—a brand-new and improved Ally.

She's moving faster and for longer, working harder. Before, she rarely took classes longer than thirty minutes, but now with Alejandro right there at her side, calling out targets tailored to her own fitness levels or how sore she's feeling that day, for the first time, she's hitting sixty-, seventy-five-, ninety-minute classes as a matter of course, ratcheting up the resistance without breaking stride, jumping in and out of the saddle like it's nothing. It's exhilarating. She's never been stronger.

And the changes aren't just apparent when she's on the bike. They're spilling over into the rest of her life, too, to all the time when she's out of the saddle. This is the best she's ever looked—she's glowing—and she knows it's not all in her head: People have started to notice her, compliment her; they seem to actually *like* her.

"I love what you've been doing with your hair," one of her coworkers tells her out of the blue.

"Have you lost weight?" another asks. "You look great."

"Yeah, there's just something about you lately," says a third.

"Tell us your secrets. And then bottle them up and *sell* them. The world has got to know."

Strangers have been holding the door open for her. Customers thank her for her help. One morning, a man in front of her in line at the coffee shop even paid for her coffee. Her coworkers have started sitting with her on lunch breaks. They included her for the first time ever in the annual Secret Santa and raved about the Team Spirit-brand insulated metal water bottle she'd given to Lorie from warehouse, passing it around with a kind of jealous appreciation, weighing its heft in their hands, noting its galactic swirl of blue and black and purple, the way the painted-on stars glinted in the store light. The other day, a few of the younger staff from the grocery department even invited her to go out with them at night, and they seemed genuinely disappointed when she told them she already had plans and turned them down.

"I can't say I wasn't flattered, and the way they're always talking about their weekends … well, I *was* tempted. But I'm afraid the time for going out is long past. It's just evenings in, some good conversation with a friend, maybe a glass or two of wine, and early to bed for me," she said to Alejandro later that evening, holding up her wineglass to him in a mock toast. "Could you even imagine, *me*, at *this* age, out drinking with a bunch of twenty-something-year-olds? What would I have worn?"

"Whenever I'm in a pinch, I find my Team Spirit apparel is always a good fit, no matter the occasion," he said with an absolutely straight face, and with a snap of his fingers, he changed into a rainbow tracksuit, the Team Spirit logo—two hands, fingers spread wide, one palm marked with a T, the other an S—emblazoned in gold across the chest. Snap. Yellow Team Spirit cycling shorts and matching close-fitting cycling jersey. Snap. Blue-and-white-striped Team Spirit footie pajamas.

How she laughed and laughed after that, and then she laughed all the harder when she glanced up to find him looking at her with puzzlement, still dressed in his Team Spirit pajamas. "Oh, Alejandro—you are an absolute gem," she told him once she finally managed to stop laughing. "What would I do without you?"

She hadn't spoken in jest—she *doesn't* know what she'll do when the thirty days are over. She's searched and searched, but she can't find any information about the trial. She sent a private message to crypticmonkey123 on SaidIt and even DMed Team Spirit tech support, but she's gotten no response from either quarter. She has no idea if or when the program will go public or how much it will cost. She is still paying off the bike, and with the Team Spirit monthly membership fee and her mother's medical and hospice bills … there is just no way she can afford to keep him around.

What she does know is that she'll be lost without him. She owes it all to Alejandro—all of the changes that the past few weeks have wrought in her—even if he's too modest to take credit for any it.

"You're the one who's putting in the work and showing up, bonanafanafofally," he told her after she tried thanking him. "I'm just along for the ride. I'm cheering you on from the sidelines. You are amazing; I hope you know that. I'm so proud of you."

Ally blushed—actually *blushed*. It was the nicest thing anyone had ever said to her.

She knows it's not *really* him, that he's not *really* there, that he's not *really* alive, and that someone has programmed this version of him into being, but she still can't shake the feeling that there's more to him than that and that even if he's not alive, he's also not *not* alive. He's something else.

"What do you get up to when I'm not around?" she asks him once in the middle of a post-class stretch, sitting up after a straddle forward fold. "What are you going to do after I leave for work?"

"You can power off your bike if you no longer wish me to be here," he says. "Let's move into downward dog and stretch out those hammies." He moves into the position. "Oof, I really needed that. If you pedal through your legs, you'll feel the stretch more deeply in your calves."

"No, no, it's not that," Ally says as she presses her palms against the mat, straightens her arms, and pushes her hips into the air. "I'm just wondering if you get bored at home, all alone. Should I try to move the TV down here or leave the radio on for you?"

Alejandro shifts from downward dog into a seated position. Ally watches him from her downward dog as she bends one knee and pushes the opposite heel down, then switches. He seems to be seriously considering her question.

"I'm sorry. I didn't understand that. Please repeat what you said or else try restarting me."

Ally sighs. "Never mind. Forget I asked. Let's just get back to stretching."

"I'm sorry. I didn't under—"

"Resume stretch," she says, more loudly this time.

Later, after she returns from work, Ally digs up the old radio from her mother's room, sets it on top of an overturned trash can near her bike, and tunes it to the local pop station. Alejandro watches her with polite interest from over near her *You Got This* sign, bobbing up and down as he does jumping jacks.

Ally moves the radio an inch to the right and takes a step back to check that it's centered. "There we go," she says. "Now you'll at least have something to keep you company when I'm not here. I just hate the thought of you all alone and with nothing to do."

Alejandro doesn't respond. He has moved on from jumping jacks to full-on, chest-to-the-floor push-ups, counting them out under his breath, each one as perfect as the one before it. Soon, Ally knows, he will proceed to mountain climbers, then burpees, on to jump squats, followed by five minutes of plank variations, then on to his back for jackknifes and bicycle crunches before starting the whole sequence again.

Ally settles down into the old, worn-out loveseat that she'd unburied from beneath a stack of boxes earlier in the week and pushed closer to the bike. On the radio, a pop star whose name she doesn't recognize croons about lost loves and the ghosts of Christmases past. Outside, the wind howls, skittering dead leaves across the pavement. Ally pulls a blanket over her legs, and over in his corner, Alejandro holds plank.

At the hospice one evening after work, on Day 29, two days before Christmas, Ally perches on the edge of her mother's bed. Her mother is tucked beneath a pile of blankets, withered to a slip of a thing, barely making a wrinkle beneath them. Outside, the gray clouds gather, heralding fresh snow.

"And how is that little friend of yours doing, this Alejandro? You haven't mentioned him even once today," her mother says. "I hope there's been no trouble in paradise."

"No, no, of course not, not at all. Nothing like that. He's been an absolute doll. He said the funniest thing just the other day," Ally says. "Oh, what was it again? I should have written it down somewhere so I could tell you."

"Our sweet boy," her mother says. "When will you bring him by to visit?"

"You know how it is. He's always so busy with work and travel. I barely see him myself. But I know he'd love to stop by to meet you if he could. Soon."

Her mother reaches a hand toward Ally's and gives it a squeeze. "All these months, I've been hating that I left you in that empty house all alone, but maybe it was for the best. It got me out of your hair," she says. "I've never seen you so happy. You must love Alejandro a lot."

The change in Ally is instantaneous, a switch flipped, and then some inner wall collapses, sending everything she has been holding back for weeks spilling out, so quickly that Ally, caught up in the deluge, hardly knows what is happening. Unbidden, tears spring to her eyes, and she is a swirl of guilt and shame and confusion. A glowing warmth surges somewhere in the region of her chest.

But before she can gather herself enough to respond, someone knocks on the door. The Friday-night nurse enters the room, today dressed in scrubs patterned with holiday-themed cats and wheeling a cart on top of which sit a stack of blue wash towels and two basins of water, plumes of steam twisting and winding in their wake.

Ally dabs at her eyes with her sleeve, the warmth still swelling there in her chest, the emotion still stinging her nose.

She clears her throat. "I should be going," Ally says as she stands to leave. "And don't forget, I'll be—"

"Working tomorrow, yes, yes, I remember. Not to worry; you'd be here if you could. I'll see you Christmas Day," her mother says, giving Ally's hand another squeeze before letting go. "Now, go on, get home before the bad weather rolls in. Besides, I've got my spa treatment tonight," she says, gesturing toward the cart.

In the parking lot, Ally sits in her frigid car, her hands pressed tight to her chest. Her heart feels as though it's grown three sizes too big; it beats faster, faster, faster, thudding steady and loud, and she tries, without hope, without reason, to slow its pace, pressing it down, pushing it back.

She'd never dared to venture down that road, hadn't put words to the feeling—but now that she's heard it, now that she's put a name to it, she knows it's the truth, and her heart is swelling, swelling with this newfound knowledge, glowing warm, reaching outward, pulling toward and in. The world grown brighter for it, sharp-hued and clear.

The minutes pass, and finally, Ally's nerves settle down. Then, slowly, she reaches for her phone. Her hands shake as she pulls up the Team Spirit app and then swipes over to her favorited classes, scans the list until she finds one of her favorite twenty-minute rides from deep in the vaults. She hits play and sets the phone down in the passenger seat.

"Hello hello hello, Team Spirit," Alejandro's voice says over the tinny speakers, and Ally is suffused with a joy like nothing she's ever known; she's overcome with it. "This is Alejandro Gutiérrez Delgado, and boy howdy, have I got a *jam-packed* class for you today—I mean, we're talking PB&J-ain't-got-nothing-on-this-class *jam-packed* …."

Outside, the snow falls fast and heavy, landing in watery splotches on the hood, on the windows, the ground. In the distance, the spray of traffic passing over wet roads; closer in, the softly fuzzed glow of the hospice's Christmas lights. Ally turns the key in the ignition, and the car sputters on. Icy air blasts through the air vents, and Ally can't contain it anymore; she is laughing, laughing at nothing, everything, the absurdity of her situation, the absurdity of her love, the hopelessness of it all, the loss that soon will come—and then, before she knows it, she is crying, weeping; she is bereft.

"Well, what are you waiting for?" Alejandro's voice continues. "Clip in those shoes already and come right on over and join me for some Team Spirit-ual healing."

When she gets home, Ally heads straight to the basement. She finds Alejandro on his bike, silently pedaling away. He does not notice her standing there behind him in the staircase. He pedals and pedals, and then he rises from his seat, sweat sheening his calves, his shoulders, the back of his neck glistening with it. Ally does not approach him or make her presence known; she does not want to intrude on him in the little time he has left. Instead, she takes a seat on the bottom step, from which she watches her friend, her coach, her love, her Alejandro.

It's the morning before Christmas, and Ally's on the road to Chicago, dressed in her green-and-red-checkered Team Spirit bike shorts and matching holiday sports bra, her lipstick the red of fresh winterberries, a ribbon of silvery white woven into her hair. She knows the look is an indulgence and, honestly, a little much, but she wants to make this day one to remember, so she'd dipped into her savings, had it all delivered express to her doorstep.

At a quarter past five, she pulls in front of a brownstone, all festooned in holiday cheer. For hours, she'd searched his social media posts and dug through property records until she'd found the address. She knows he'll be there, that she's at the right one.

In the rearview mirror, by the glow of the streetlight, she checks her hair and makeup, then adjusts the right leg of her shorts, which has ridden up.

Within her, a nervous energy twists around and around; she ignores it, pushes it away. She thinks instead of her mother, of her coworkers, of her bike in the basement at home, the Ally she was, the Ally she's become. She knows she's taking a risk, but this is her only hope.

"You *got* this," she says aloud, her skin goosebumped with cold. "*I* got this. *I* can."

A few minutes 'til the hour, and she opens her door. It's time; she's ready to go. Soon, she'll see him, live in his home: Alejandro Gutiérrez Delgado, coiffed and shined and pressed and primped. Together, they'll pedal. Together, they'll work, Ally and Alejandro, Alejandro and Ally, forever side by side.

Denise Duhamel

Crawling

The first song I ever wrote was "Come Crawling"
in which I begged a lover to come back—*come crawling,*
come crawling is all you have to do. I was in sixth grade.
What did I know about love's betrayal? The "you"
in my song was a cheater, though I hadn't been cheated on,
not yet. The "I" was giving the "you" a second chance.
I've only written a few other songs, all unremarkable.
The best was a collaboration with Hugh. We called it
"Lonely Couple" and invoked the spirit of my dead uncle.
Hugh had a great voice and played the guitar.
There were so many bands in our Boston college days
getting airtime, we must have thought *why not us?*
I was shy except when I was drunk and the drunker
I became, the more off-key. Once, at a house party,
I jumped on someone's bed, playing an air-flute
and singing a song I wrote on the spot as I went along.
I had no memory of it the next day, even when my friends
tried to recreate my lyrics. A little rocker
living deep inside me must have wanted to be
Chrissie Hynde, but the rest of my body couldn't cooperate.
I turned to poetry not realizing someday, if I succeeded,
I'd have to do poetry readings. Hugh became
a social worker and the friend on whose bed I sang
and used as a stage moved to Amsterdam. Back then,
my favorite album was The Pretenders' *Learning to Crawl*.
I recently found my music book from my days
of teenage accordion lessons. In it, on the first page
is "Denise's Song," no words, just neat painstaking notes
written in purple pen, crawling across the page.

Denise Duhamel

Jim

lived next door to my mother where his grass
was full of knee-high weeds. Mice had started
to make nests in his yard. Rumors were he was
in foreclosure, maybe living somewhere in his car.
Jim used to help my mom—clip her shrubs
and roll her garbage bins to the curb. His own garage
was full of old TVs and VCRs, microwaves,
an extra toilet. When my father was alive,
he would talk to Jim. My father liked eccentrics
and, besides, Jim knew the street's
gossip. Now Jim was the gossip. He didn't
have a wife or children or any relatives
we knew about. His house was dark
and we speculated his electricity was shut off.
My mother had already grown leery of Jim.
She said he wasn't right in the head.
When she could still cook, she made him
plates of food but at some point grew afraid
to knock on his door. Social services kept looking
for Jim, leaving notes. My mother went
into the nursing home before I learned
his story. All I know is what I can see.
His grass is fertilized, green, the weeds
pulled up. His garage door is down.
Who knows who lives in Jim's house now.

Brian Simoneau

Joke Without a Punchline

Why did the dipshit cross the road in the dark?
    A priest, a thief, and a dipshit stood on a bridge.
How many lies does a dipshit tell his wives at night?
    How many dipshits does it take to bake an apple pie?

A dipshit and a bag of bones walk into a bar.
    How many casinos can a dipshit own?
Why did the dipshit go broke again and again?
    What do you call a gun in a dipshit's pocket?

Why did the dipshit pour coal slurry down the well?
    What do you call a dipshit in a pinstriped suit?
What did the dipshit say about the poisoned flock?

    How does a dipshit sound like an empty church?
Why did the villagers burn the dipshit's cottage down?
    What's the difference between a village and smoldering ash?

Brian Simoneau

In My Latest Dream of Freddie Mercury

the red-capped gawkers on the mall, slack-jawed
and silent, stared between banners and flags
as the justice presiding shucked his robes
and there he was, strutting like Montreal
1981—no grand piano
holding his plastic cups, no microphone
scepter-swung, he swaggered downstage to take
from a roadie an acoustic guitar
and wielding it like a sword, battle ax,
the fascist-killing machine it was once,
smashed it against the leather-bound ledger
the would-be sovereign had planned to swear on
and a voice rang out from the dome above,
a call to prayer, dirge for what we've become.

Ruth Joffre

A Girl Gets Lost

This was back when weekends meant trips to the mall so your little brother could get new tennis shoes and your mom could go to her hair appointment while your dad peppered the staff at Best Buy with increasingly technical questions about color temperature on the latest television in stock or back-ordered for the holidays; back when you almost enjoyed ambling from store to store with a diet soda, peering into the lightning balls and flipping through the latest comics while you willed yourself not to walk past Auntie Anne's or beg your mom for cinnamon-sugar pretzels. Of course she wouldn't buy you one—you knew that—but sometimes you walked by anyway just to picture yourself there, with a pretzel in one hand and a purse in the other, like older women at the food court. Sometimes, you took tallies of their lives: three kids, two shopping bags, one halfway decent-looking husband; or two kids, one stroller, and some brand of toy gun that shot foam darts or pellets; or no kids at all, just a pretzel and a book with crisp new pages. You never understood how you—a child, a thirteen-year-old who had never handled more than twenty dollars in cash—were supposed to become this person who spends her Saturday returning shirts and buying radios with waterproof chassis so she could listen to music in the shower. What choices would you have to make to become that person? What steps were between Point A and Point B? You didn't know them then and couldn't imagine taking them, even if you did. After six hours at the mall, you just wanted someone to show you where to go and what to do. Maybe that was why you followed the young man pushing a dolly loaded with delivery boxes, and maybe that was why, when he turned down a long hallway you had never noticed before, your curiosity got the better of you and made you turn with him, away from the food court, far from the Auntie Anne's, into an area of the mall you never imagined existed, full of broken-down animatronics and deconstructed booths from the decades of restaurant renovations already undertaken. You didn't think there was space for more. The entire storeroom was filled to the brim with lamps, milk crates, bookshelves, deep fryers, the names of stores you didn't even recognize (Lansburgh's, Hecht's, Jelleff's). Cobwebs forced you to duck, and dust prompted you to sneeze so viciously you were afraid someone would catch you skulking around—that delivery man, maybe, though you hadn't seen him in some time now. You don't know how long you were in that room. It seemed like twenty minutes, but, when you left, it was dark in the hallway. A skylight illuminated what was left of the food court—its derelict stalls, its overgrown flowerpots and mossy benches. You liked the way they felt. So soft. So alive.

Ruth Joffre

A Girl Next Door

You can't help thinking that she reminds you of someone. Maybe it's the way she holds a pink ribbon between her teeth as she pulls her blond hair back in a ponytail, just like Mrs. Nowak from down the street used to do before going on a run, before losing her hair to chemotherapy; or maybe it's that song she half-hums while watering flowers in the front yard, the song that jangles inside you like a quarter in a slot machine, unlocking old memories of being put to bed as a child by your babysitter, Mrs. Miller, who lived three streets over and sang the most beautiful lullabies until a tracheostomy permanently altered her voice and her daughter placed her in assisted living; or perhaps it's the scent of baked apple and cinnamon always wafting from her kitchen, the scent you first encountered at a neighborhood potluck, years ago, when the widow Winnie was still the best baker on the block, regularly serving up apple coffee cakes and lemon tarts and these perfect little peppermint meringues until the dementia finally caught up with her and all her recipes were lost—all but this one, which the girl next door bakes every Saturday like clockwork, even though her parents must be sick of it by now; then again, it could also be the way she sometimes looks at you (you, with your nonexistent thigh gap and your tattoo of a lion's head on your left arm; you, who have only ever received one compliment about your looks from your grandmother, who said you had inherited your father's good teeth, thank the Lord); for some reason, that girl looks at you like you have something she must have, like you once looked at the pretty girls at school, at their fashionable haircuts and exquisitely shaped noses, the way they swanned through the department store where you worked, until one day you couldn't take it anymore and stuffed a pair of jeans in your bag without checking the tag, then walked home, hot faced, wondering what ever possessed you to want to be like anyone else; you never stole again, but you have no idea what the girl next door is capable of doing to get what she wants. All you know is your teeth hurt. All of them.

Abby Manzella

Castoffs

Bridget, in her turquoise swimming suit and gym shorts, ducks beneath the public pool's deck. She is looking for the quarter that slipped from her clutches, rolled along the deck, and escaped through the wooden slats. That flooring, now transformed into Bridget's three-foot high ceiling, forces her to crouch. Her goal is to reunite this lost coin with its matching partners in her pocket so that she can exchange them all for an ice cream sandwich, like her friends do, their dollars so easily gliding across the snack bar.

Her eyes quickly adjust to the darkness, which is diminished by thin lines of daylight that seep through the overhead boards. She is striped by these beams—a prisoner behind translucent bars no matter where she moves. As Bridget searches, scraping herself on things unseen, the strap of her suit slips. The one-piece is big, inherited from her cousin's outgrown shelf, but Bridget is proud of the color, like a sunlit gem.

Pretty as a peacock, her mother said. *You'll grow into it*, she reassured.

Bridget spies the gleam of her quarter, just as she hears Addison above, taking a seat at their favorite table. Others follow. The scuffing noise of rearranging chairs reverberates around Bridget's head. All she has to do is creep those last few feet to rescue her quarter.

At first, it is the tone of gossip that refocuses Bridget's attention from her lost coin to her friend. Addison has taken up a rundown of "Who wears it best?" Reed stands out in his board shorts and Kayla in a one-shoulder suit. Then, as Bridget finishes her slow scramble toward her change, she hears what she has long feared: her name followed by laughter. *Faded*, one says. *Stretched out*, says another. They share their criticism lightly, passing it from one girl to the next. It is a cruel hand-me-down.

Bridget shrinks into herself; she wishes she had a cover-up to hide her shame. The hazy grayness of the stifled light weighs upon her—she feels both unseen and exposed. She makes not a noise when she reaches for her quarter, which she clasps hard, no longer as a treasure but as a ratty security blanket. Once she accomplishes her mission, she makes no further moves; she is hunched and still. The giggling persists, leaving the undetected girl beneath their feet with a feeling she'll never discard.

Abby Manzella

The Puzzle Piece

There is a puzzle piece missing, just like Jackie's baby tooth. At first, when the policemen return him to his father's arms, Jackie doesn't notice the lacking jigsaw fragment. But once the adults forget about him, he spies the absence—the final piece of sky above the daffodil-filled field. Jackie squirms from his father's grasp. The piece, unlike his front tooth, hadn't wiggled or bled after its fall. It's just gone. He peers around the chairs and then crawls under the table.

At the day's start, he presented his wrenched-out tooth to his mother. She clapped.

"You're growing up!" She'd said before whispering, "The Tooth Fairy is sure to come and give you a gift in exchange for your tooth."

Now, he runs his tongue through the new gap, tender and fleshy. Maybe the Tooth Fairy won't come.

Earlier, his mother drove him to the mall to celebrate.

"Ice cream cones, my fuzzy bunny boy. It's fun to lick when you've lost a tooth."

Jackie liked Rocky Road the best.

The void in the laminated cardboard is shaped like a person with four limbs. The feet and hands, if they were there, would be shaped like hearts. One knob for the head and three blanks all around—the language of puzzles that his mother taught him as they played. He mostly announced the colors. Jackie can feel his heart beating in his exposed gum.

Jackie was left in the cavity of the wreckage for hours before the men found him and pried him out. Jackie and his mother had been singing in the car, and then they weren't. Spun, twisted, yanked into nothingness. He cried the name he always cried. No one responded.

The adults blather on, but from Jackie's low angle, he can't see them. Without his mommy, how will he do puzzles? Will he get a new tooth or will that stay gone, too? She told him that some things come back like flowers in the spring but not his goldfish. Nibbles also disappeared, and the bowl sat filled with water but no fish. Jackie stared through the clearness to the colors on its other side. The objects were warped but still there.

For now, he stays hidden beneath the table, searching for that final piece of blue. He will place it and his tooth under his pillow. He will hope for something to return in their place.

Summer Hammond

(I Won't Know, Until Later)

In the foothills of the Ozarks, twilight is an enchantment.

That sounds like a fairy tale.

And since it cost more than you can fathom to be here, sitting cross-legged in the grass, waiting for Dane to bring me an iced lemonade, I need this to be a fairy tale.

(I won't know, until later, that daughters like me are chronic dreamers with the lifelong tendency to alchemize fear and anguish into fantasy.)

I tear at grass, the most self-soothing activity, and gaze at the dark and rumpled, the small wrinkles of mountains, parading like shadows across the purpling sky. A breeze moves through, and the pines sing. When pines sing and there are foothills in the distance, foothills beckoning, you are apt to forget that your mother threw the cake stand at you.

Dane emerges from the barn, a red cup in each hand. As he strides toward me, a fiddle yowls like a wild cat, and inside, the boots, all those boots, stomp out a fierce, a free, a thunderous, joyful chorus.

To dance like that, you have to let go. Your muscles have to surrender their prized guardianship of your tender organs. You have to let the fiddle reach right through your cells, warm and inviting, pick up your bones and play them.

You can't be afraid.

You mustn't be imagining your mother's face, the red snarl of it, as she heaves her most beloved cake stand at the wall and it bursts, chillingly, near your head.

(I won't know, until later, about personality disorders and that mothers can have them, and if your mother has borderline personality disorder, for instance, it's possible something very terrible happened to her very early, stunting her developmentally, and the tantrums of a two-year-old manifested in a fifty-year-old are terrifying.)

I wonder how many girls are here tonight, in the foothills of the Ozarks, on their first date, like runaways, like convicts, locked in a sweaty terror over the prospect of returning home.

This is the kind of mental calculation I've done all my life. Always ending up with the same number.

One.

Dane crouches beside me on the cool grass, hands me a cup. "Thank you," I say. The cup is chilled and quiets my hand, which hasn't fully stopped trembling since I jumped into his old blue pickup and we rattled away together down the gravel lane.

Dane doesn't answer, just raises his cup.

He is the grill cook at the small-town-Missouri McDonald's where we work.

I'd venture he is the serenest grill cook in the world. No fussing. No cursing. No fit-throwing. No grill-cook drama.

Just the special order slid down the warming bin and your name, softly called.

"Thea. Big Mac, extra pickle, extra sauce." Simple as that.

He brought me here and I never knew this place was here. Lit-up barn, tucked into the backwoods, glittering and crying out music. I've spent so much time alone with books.

How many Narnias are there—so near yet hidden from me?

I'm looking at Dane, pondering this, when I see. The dimple in his chin. His strong jaw. The pieces of him falling together in a way they haven't before, creating an image I *know*. The shock of recognition straightens my spine.

"Dane," I say. "You're *Dane*."

Think about it. I've worked with him for three months and didn't remember—.

His smile is gentle. "Yes. That's me. I'm Dane."

"You're Dane."

"I am."

"*Dane*. From American history!" I throw grass on his knee.

He glances at the grass. At me. "History?"

"Ninth grade. Mr. Potter. Remember?"

He nods, takes a swig of lemonade. Doesn't brush the grass away.

"That was you, wasn't it?"

"Might've been." His grin is crooked.

"I'm Thea. Thea Woods."

He squints at my face.

"Thea! The new girl. The one with the odd cloud of hair." I pat my hair for confirmation, and sharp bits pierce my palm. *Glass.*

If he sees the horror on my face, he doesn't say.

Dane stands, jogs off, and when he comes back, he offers me a horseshoe.

It gleams, a perfect, poignant curl of silver—like a small slice of the moon.

I have to clean up the cake stand before I go to bed.

No one's touched it.

It's been left for me.

The pieces lay scattered, glinting like teeth.

Shark teeth. Or maybe magic wolves.

Everything can become a fairy tale in my head, if I let it.

And picking up tooth after tooth of broken glass, setting it in the dustpan, I recall:

> 1. This is the cake stand Ruby and I bought her not long after she admired it in the antique shop but bemoaned her lack of money. It is—*was*—baroque glass, a dusky pink. In secret, Ruby and I combined our meager savings, and when the shopkeeper wrapped it for us, she did so with entrancing care, rolling the cake stand, enfolding it in layer upon layer of special wrap, the color of a deer, at last binding it with twine, easing it into a bag that Ruby would sneak into the car then into the house, concealing it in the back of her closet. The treasure my sister and I shared between us, presented to our mother with streamers and singing, I could never imagine would end up a rupture of glass, an echo in my ears, brokenness caught inside my hair the night of my first date.
>
> 2. I had not been nice to Dane in ninth grade American History. I was the new girl, and I hurt him. Back then, he was short. Even shorter than I was. He

> wore the hat, the boots, the tight jeans. But with thick glasses and his face, equally thick with pimples. One day, a classmate boisterously suggested that *the Yankee new girl* be escorted to homecoming by *the nerd cowboy* who sat in front of her. Dane looked round at me, over his shoulder, his smile both shy and hopeful. I noted the whiskers sprouting from his zits. And I said, "Ew." This was a jolt, like grabbing hold of electric barbed wire. That I had said, *Ew*, out loud. Dane swallowed hard, a terrible storm of red creeping up his neck, saturating his face. Tugging the brim of his cowboy hat over his eyes, he whipped away. His pain crashed over me in waves the rest of the day.

I crouch on the kitchen floor, juggling these two memories.
Between my fingers, the last shard.
What was once so precious, now a fang.

In the morning, I take a breath, knock.

She says, "What do you want."

That's as good as *Come on in*! and I tingle with hope.

I open her door. Her room is dark. She's in bed, a chaotic topography sprawled beneath the covers.

I whisk off my McDonald's visor, crush it to my heart. "Mom. I'm sorry."

"Oh, you are, huh?" She sweeps the covers away like a theater curtain parting to reveal the star. "I was baking you a cake," she spits. "And you *left* me." She pounds her fist to her chest. Deep, sickening thuds.

Betrayal. Abandonment. Dagger driven through her heart.

(I won't know, until later, that narcissism is the mechanism of a shattered ego protecting itself, and mothers can have this, too, and if so, they might feel profoundly threatened, rejected, by a daughter's independence-seeking, particularly if they've been enmeshed with each other.)

Her face shakes with passion, conviction, as she points at me. "*You.*"

That one word. The hatefulness of my being. The fakery of my fuzzy ponytail. The lie of my blue McDonald's polo shirt, black trouser pants, and nonslip restaurant shoes.

She says, "Want to know something? I was sooo happy." She leans forward in bed, ponytail twisted sideways like a broken limb, and claps her hands to emphasize each word. "*Just. So. Happy.* When that redneck's nasty old blue pickup truck came to get you!"

She throws her head back and laughs.

Hahaha!

The tables at McDonald's will never be cleaner as I lean in, try to scrub the echo of my mother's laughter from my mind.

The lunch crew arrives. Casey storms in, complaining that her mother has grounded her.

Lydia pries. "What'd you do this time, you little hussy?" She smacks Casey on the butt with a cleaning rag.

Casey jumps and hoots. "Wouldn't you like to know!"

"Oh, I bet I can guess." Lydia wink-wink-winks behind her round tortoiseshell glasses. We call her Captain Drive-Thru. She is the best at it, never makes mistakes. She graduated college with an art degree. She lives with her parents and uses her McDonald's paychecks to buy painting supplies.

Lydia calls to Casey, "Does that mean you can't come out clubbing with me tonight?"

"Two weeks!" Casey yells from the back.

"Aw, well. Shoot." Lydia stomps around, restocking the ketchup and mustard bins. "What about you, Venus? You and Cowboy do some boot-stompin' boogie last night?" She whistles through her teeth.

Lydia calls me Venus because she says I am the spitting image of the goddess in a painting she loves called *The Birth of Venus*. A melancholy beauty.

I don't answer. I'm thinking about grounding. The exotic wonder of it. To break a rule. To do something bad. Something conventionally agreed upon as bad—sneaking out, imbibing, sex and drugs. And to be punished for it, coolly, firmly, as a matter of parental responsibility.

My mother has not ever grounded me. If anyone knew that, they might think me preternaturally blessed.

I look around McDonald's and wonder who in here, right now, what girl, what daughter, is punished with frenzy and frothing at the mouth? With despair and rage and breakage? All the pieces of her mother, fractured flesh, glinting at her feet and howling, laughing.

The calculation is, of course, unchanging.

One.

I arrive home to breaking news.

Ruby informs me, "Mom moved into the RV."

Ruby tells me this while studying in her room.

She looks up from her notebook, says, "I've never made Mom move into the RV."

I have out-badded Ruby, and that is something neither of us ever expected.

That is because I am the good one. *The Good One.*

Ruby, biting her lip, jabs her calculator. Mother and Sister—two warring countries I was born between, oblivious, bald, and colicky. Ruby is the small country with quaint weaponry who nonetheless sneers in the face of the Big Dog, the one with nuclear firepower at its fingertips. I've witnessed, through the years, my sister being screamed at, smacked, hair wrenched back, reviled, a final splintering punch thrown at her door, the bash, left there in the wood. A testament to warfare. Rather than cover it up with a poster, as I would, Ruby got out her paints, painted it scarlet—amplifying and turning into a monument that cavernous, splintered hole.

Only then did Dad take notice. He bought Ruby a new door, seamlessly replaced the old, quietly toted it to some dumpster, disposed of it without a word about the garishly decorated fist smash.

Ruby says that through education, she is digging herself a tunnel to freedom—perfect attendance, perfect grades, perfect GPA. Perfection is her new survival tactic, amulet, and way out.

She hunches, zealously working out a calculus equation in a notebook. In one corner of her desk, notecards laden with French vocabulary, neatly stacked. In the other corner, a pile of books: *Collected Poems of Edna St. Vincent Millay*, *The Madwoman in the Attic*, *A Room of One's Own*.

Wuthering Heights. She's reading that one for the third time.

I note that her copy, unlike mine, is littered with sticky notes.

She's also taking a sculpture class. She arrives home, some nights, in dusty overalls. She's working on a bust, the most intimate form of sculpture, she says. A portrait of herself.

"Isn't that weird?" I'd asked her. "Pounding and chiseling at your own head?"

The look she gave, dark. "Better to pound and chisel at my own head than let anyone else."

Mom says Ruby is disloyal, doesn't care, can't be trusted. *The Bad One.*

(I won't know, until later, that Ruby and I have been psychologically pitted against one another, the Golden Child versus the Scapegoat, and this will chisel our heads, our very relationship, into irredeemable smithereens, from which we will never recover, never know, on this Earth, how we might have loved each other.)

I say, "Mom moved into the RV because of me?"

And Ruby answers with a smirk, a wag of her head. "Alas, dear sister! It's *your* turn."

The next morning, I stumble through the dark laundry room on my way to work.

Numb. In a stupor. A *my-mother-has-moved-into-the-RV* hangover.

I swing open the door to the garage, and—my mother steps onto the top step in her bathrobe at the same time I step down.

We meet, freeze, lock eyes.

She recoils.

Draws back with horror, like she's met with a cobra.

The one who conceived and held me in her body.

The one who endured untold pain to bring me here.

I wonder how she looked at me the first time she held me in her arms?

Because the way she looks at me now—drawing her blue robe tight, lips pulling back, teeth bared, eyes narrowed and pupils black—I am speared by her hate.

Lydia whips the dish towel at me with a snap. I flinch, jump back.

Nothing I can do about the tears. They are a mob. An unstoppable swarm.

Lydia peers at me. "What's the matter, Venus? I spank you too hard?" Then, with a laugh that's not so brazen, she falters. "You and Cowboy have a spat? Need me to teach him a lesson?" She grinds her fist into her palm.

Lydia, has your mother ever looked at you with hate?

The question is poised like a diver on the tip of my tongue.

I slump with relief when a car pulls into the drive-thru and off she marches, shoulders back. "Welcome to McDonald's. May I take your order, please?" The consoling chant of those words.

But, it doesn't end there.

I want, with chaotic desperation, to grab every customer by the shirt collar. Want to shake them, make them answer.

When your mother gets mad at you, what does she do?

I tap the register keys.

I make drinks, soda erupting, whooshing like a geyser.

I hand over fries, trays laden with neatly wrapped, grease-slick burgers.

Have you ever made your mother move into the RV?

My eyes sweep the restaurant. A worn-out trucker dozes, head back against the booth, dirty ball cap pulled over his face. An old man in overalls licks an ice cream cone, glued to the weather channel on the TV in the corner. A teenage girl plays with a Happy Meal toy, her friends giggling up a storm as she dances Sleeping Beauty around their milkshakes, up to their lips, begging for a kiss.

Why must I keep doing this math?

(I won't know, until later, that there are untold numbers of us, a whole tribe, carrying the stories of our mothers in silence, because having a mother like ours is taboo, and there are no Mother's Day cards that tell our story, so that even if our utter aloneness is not the truth, it continues to feel like ….)

One. One. One.

It is near midnight. Her third night in the RV.

Dad knocks on Ruby's bedroom door, then mine.

Waking us, he whispers for us to follow him.

We do as we are told, my sister and I, stumbling outside in our shorts and tees, hastily sliding on flip-flops, into the warm luxury of a soft early-summer night in the Ozarks.

The stars are a feast.

We walk together, circling the house.

We circle the house, in silence, three times.

I wonder why Ruby and I submit to this. Perhaps other daughters, in their different kinds of families, would be startled, rattled, freaked, by this midnight summons, this wordless jaunt. Perhaps they would resist, refuse to get up, decline the invitation to follow their father around the yard, waiting for the words to start. They might, at least, ask questions.

(I won't know, until later, that the routine subjection to coercive control, a repertoire of manipulative behaviors meant to punish and demoralize victims back in line, results in chronically low self-efficacy and the erosion of one's backbone into a vertebral sand.)

Ruby and I shuffle-kick through the grass, rub our arms against the mounting dread.

Each time we pass the RV, I stare at the darkened windows, willing my heart to touch hers.

Dad stops us on the fourth enforced march, by the front porch, near the swing he made for us when we first moved to the Ozarks. He'd been delirious with hope that we would sit together, a *Country Living* family, and relish these star-soaked summer nights in the foothills. The swing now creaks in a breeze. Its slats gleam white and bare, a skeleton's grin.

Dad says, "I have a plan."

My ears perk. Dad is smart. Dad studied civil engineering. He was in the last semester of his senior year when he dropped out to marry mom.

Dad says, "Next time around, we'll stop outside the RV. We'll talk. We'll argue. I'll throw punches at you and start to kick—"

Ruby gasps. "You'll *what*?"

"I'll pretend to attack you," Dad says. "Hopefully, this will activate her maternal instinct. She'll rush outside to save you."

Ruby shakes her head. She backs up.

"Imagine we're performing a skit."

I look between them, Dad so earnest and Ruby aghast. I try to decide what to feel.

Dad barks, "Do you want your mother to move back in or don't you?"

(I won't know, until later, that dad is an enabler driven to mollify and protect the coercive controller at all costs, which also makes him complicit.)

Ruby backs and backs, all the way into one of the spirea she pruned and trimmed this spring. I remember her, bedecked in her big, straw hat and gardening gloves, clipping and clipping with painstaking care as though it were her art. Now, Ruby backs into the spirea and keeps going, keeps moving away, crushing the plant, all its tiny purple flowers.

You can hear snapping sounds.
Little bird wings, breaking.

On the rink, the following night, Dane takes my hand.

I try to feel it, his skin and my skin, through the thick fog of shock.

Overnight, she left. She packed the car and left.

She's done many things, but she has never left.

I look down at our hands, fingers entwined.

No boy has ever, at any time, held my hand.

The lights revolve around us, changing colors, whirling slow, and holding hands, we skate off into the galaxy.

I've worn my hair down, and it lifts, it floats. My hair, a feathery concoction. And this time, neon disco lights rather than splinters of a shattered cake stand are caught inside it.

A little boy skates up behind us. "Hey!" he calls.

Dane and I turn. Our hands, shyly, part ways.

"Hey," the boy says to me. "Can I touch your hair?"

"Yes," I say.

My mother has left. I don't know where she's gone.

Everything in the world is strange, surreal, like being trapped in a psychedelic bubble.

(I won't know, until later, that psychological shock is akin to electrocution. It zaps the psyche, creates a dissociative trance between you and reality. While protective, this also prevents you from fully experiencing the surprise and pleasure of a second date, the beauty and wonder of the first time holding hands.)

The boy pets my hair. He smiles. "Wow. It's soft. Like a baby chick!" He dashes around us, careens off on his skates.

Dane takes up my hand again. He presses it, lightly, with care.

As the song winds down, I say to him: "Do you remember me, really? Thea Woods from ninth-grade History?" Before I'm too attached, I have to give him another opportunity to reject me. "I think … I was kind of mean?"

Dane smiles. That dimple of his, deepening. He reaches out, lets his hand slowly drift down my hair. "Can't imagine you being mean, Thea."

It just melts me.

More than the handholding or the caress.

His faith in my goodness—makes my knees go weak.

☾

Lydia calls in sick and the managers are flabbergasted.

In three years, Captain Drive-Thru has never missed a day of work.

I inherit her headset for the day.

Welcome to McDonald's. May I take your order, please?

The refrain I've heard Lydia sing daily, I now pick up on her behalf. It soothes the raw and badly scraped feeling inside.

At around 3 p.m., dead time, a lady pulls through in a pretty dark-green car, glossy as nail polish. She has loads of billowy auburn hair, a luxurious bosom, and theatrical makeup, as though on her way to perform at the Grand Ole Opry.

When she takes the bag from me, her gaze lingers. "Why, heavens. Look at those eyes! Darlin', what color are your eyes?"

"Sometimes blue, sometimes green, sometimes gray." *Spook eyes*, Ruby calls them, *mood rings lodged in your orbital sockets.*

"Oh baby, you are just sublime. The loveliest! You know that?"

A bizarre movie plays in my head, one where I crawl out the drive-thru window and into her car. I curl up beside her, and she feeds me honey. The kind in the glass jar on the windowsill. The kind that fills up, that glows amber with morning light.

"You ever thought about modeling, Sug-boog?"

I am about to let loose from my skin, fly around like a little star-winged butterfly.

"I knew Jesus sent me here today for a reason. Here, sweets. Here's my business card." She holds it, pinched between her fingers like a cigarette. I lean out the drive-thru window to take it. "My name's Daphne. And Thea," a quick glance at my nametag, "the Lord sent me here today on purpose to ease your sad and weary heart and make your sweetest dreams come true."

The night finds me perched on a stool in the center of Daphne's living room.

She's decorated her space in creams and whites, and in the lamp light, it is like we are on the moon together.

Daphne tells me all about Mary Kay and Jesus Christ.

I don't mind, because her fingers are on my skin. Her fingers, massaging in the cool, creamy foundation. Beforehand, she'd removed her rings, carefully, laying each one with a soft clink on the coffee table. "Don't want to hurt you now," she'd said. My chest ached with the tenderness.

She smooths the liquid across my acne scars with deliberate delicacy, as though they are sacred ground.

This … is ecstatic heaven.

More so, to me, than the kind she's talking about.

"Sug-boog, my Lord Jesus does everything for a reason, and I promise you this: He's the one brought us together today. Just think on it. You don't ever work the drive-thru. I don't ever get fast food. But, we did today, darlin'. We surely did."

Daphne's perfume is an intoxicant. Her blouse rustles, and her perfume drifts to me, drenching and dizzying as lilacs, my mother's favorite on a May evening after a nice rain.

(I won't know, until later, that this is called filial imprinting, and I will be susceptible to this form of falling in love my whole life.)

"Yes," I say. "Jesus brought us together." I've never worn foundation in my life. Nor gone to church.

When she finishes applying the foundation and her hand leaves, I nearly grab it, nearly cry out, *Come back!*

She does. She pops open a compact with little squares of eyeshadow and leans in so close, I taste in my own mouth the sweetness of the strawberry gum she snaps. She says, "Since we're in harmony that this is God's plan for you, tonight, after your free makeover, I'll show you everything I used and what you can buy. After that, we'll start training. I'll teach you all the tricks of the trade. Then, you'll be pinned. On your way to a pink Cadillac and a brand-new life! No more McDonald's, girl. How does that sound?"

"Sounds wonderful." *Daphne.* Her name is like a pillow, like a dove.

She's caressing my eyelids. The skin there, like a baby's.

So fragile, it could tear.

I turn my key in the door at 11 p.m.

I have never come home so late.

With mom, would never dare.

But mom's not here.

It is Ruby who meets me in the hallway. Ruby who takes my shoulders, leans in, and squints. "What the hell happened to your face?"

"A free makeover," I say.

"Courtesy of who? Tammy Faye?"

"Stop. You don't get it. It was amazing." I hold up a bag. Seventy-five dollars' worth of Mary Kay makeup.

"Sure, Thea. Sure it was."

"No, really," I say as she steers me toward the bathroom, "you don't even know, Ruby. It was—it is—"

She stands me in front of the bathroom mirror. The light in there is bright, a merciless truth-teller. It tells me that:

The foundation on my face is the color of … pantyhose.

The blush—like two pink clamshells punched me.

My eyelids—purple, like they've also received a wallop.

"Love," I say.

In the morning, I sit in the dark kitchen, alone at the dining-room table in my McDonald's uniform, reading *Wuthering Heights.*

The night before, after a thorough face-washing, Ruby had shoved the book in my hands.

Her copy. The one littered with sticky notes.

"But I've read it," I told her.

"Read it again."

"Why?"

"Read it until you get it."

"What?"

"Read it until you're not stupid."

I started to cry. "Are you coldhearted? Don't you miss her, Ruby? Don't you want her back? No matter what, she's our mother. *Mommy.* Mom."

Ruby, falling back on her bed, her arm flying across her forehead in a swoon. "Oh, Heathcliff! Oh, you sexy madman! You necessary and glorious abuser! You vile violent villainous victim, I'd die for you, kill my soul to save yours, let my father kick and punch me to please, to mollify your cruelty and activate your love, I would, I would, I would!"

"Stop, Ruby! Why are you being that way? So weird and hateful!"

Sitting up, folding her hands beneath her chin like a prayer. Fluttering her eyelashes and reciting, in the high-pitched sing song of some horror-movie doll, "*Whatever souls are made of, his and mine are the same.*"

Mocking me. Of that, I was sure.

I sit in the dark kitchen, alone, reading page after page then lifting my head to look.

I sit alone at the dining room table, and I look.

I look first at the spot in the middle of the table, where the erstwhile cake stand had enjoyed a whole two year's glorious, peaceful reign before meeting its bitter, embattled end.

I then look at every last plate arranged meticulously on the shelves Dad built for her.

The dining room is, I realize, a museum of my mother's plates.

Plates painted with farm scenes, with roosters and hens, sheep and cows and pigs, tractors and hay bales. Plates for every season. Spring plates hand-painted with violets. Summer plates bedecked with sunflowers, bees, and butterflies. Fall plates brilliant with pumpkins and gourds, scarecrows and bright, perfect leaves. Winter plates with horses; sleds; sleigh bells; sweet, smiling snowmen; and owls tucked into snowcapped pines.

If you saw her collection of plates—you'd think we were a family of ten.

A jolly clan. Hearty and lively. Rose-cheeked.

Living on a farm.

The house, a joyous uproar.

If you were to look at the plates.

And not at the chair with the three broken legs—that sits upside down on the screened in porch.

The splintered wood, where the legs broke off, like torn-up sinew and dried-out flesh.

I remember the smash, the impact, the bits flying out, my arm flying over my eyes, ducking, crying out, quaking there on the floor. Though that time, the rage was for Ruby.

Dad is still trying to fix the chair.

Hasn't yet.

Cake stand, my heart—all the king's horses and all the king's men,

Still couldn't.

Lydia sweeps around my feet then across my nonslip shoes, waking me. She still isn't feeling well. She's grumpy and short-fused.

She looks me in the eye, a sneer curling the edge of her lips. "What are you standing around dreaming about?"

My mother, I want to say.

Lydia's headset beeps, and she thrusts the broom at me. "Here, lazy bones. You do it. You sweep up the goddamn filth."

This is something my mother might say, with just that snap of the jaws. And I find rest in it, comfort, like a lullaby.

While I am sweeping, the restaurant doors push open.

He smiles when he sees me, waves. My heart expands. *Third date.*

I set the broom against the wall, glide to my register, stand there, beaming.

Then I see her.

The girl who's with him.

She is a prairie flower. Tall, lithe, with hair long and straight, sandy, framing a freckled face. T-shirt, tight jeans, cowboy boots. She is a prairie flower with every petal in place. Hair, teeth, hips, lips. A mother who loves her.

And they look more than good together.

They look … just right.

I meet her gaze. "What can I get for you?"

"Just a drink," she says. "A large Sprite."

"On me," Dane says. Like a gentleman, he slides two bills from his wallet. I take them, and I'm proud of my hands. Two brave souls who, when faced with a crisis, maintain their dignity, do not quake. "Large Coke for me," he says. "Light ice. Well, you know what I like." And when he says it, he winks. Not with scorn or malice. Just simple. Just sweet.

My head spins as I make the drinks. Yet, I ensure they are well made. Beautiful. Full to the top. *Sprite, no spite.* I place the lids carefully, secure them, each crinkling edge, so they don't spill. I hand hers to her so our fingers touch, all the while smiling. *Sprite, no spite.*

Ringing them up, diligently adding the employee discount, no stone of careful kindness left unturned, I notice the camera on a woven strap, hearts and sunflowers, around her neck. I tell her, "Wow, that's a beautiful camera."

She lifts it up, says, "Thanks! I plan to get some good shots. Dane's being romantic, taking me to see an old barn. I'm a sucker for things like that. I love falling-apart things."

I swallow. "I do, too."

I wave at them as they leave.

"Is that how it works?" I cry. "Dating?"

Daphne circles me, massaging moisturizer into my skin. I paid $50 for this moisturizer. In truth, I paid for her to touch me, to tell me the truths that only women know and pass to other women. Though I vowed to Ruby I would not return here again, here I am. Daphne leans in close, two fingers sweeping through the pricey jar. "Oh, sweets. I don't know …."

"Did this ever happen to you?"

"Well, no. It seems weird. You went on two dates and then he brings in a new girl. It's almost like … he was out to get you. But, that can't be true, now, can it?"

Ew.

I bang my heels against the stool. "I ew'd him! One time. Only once, in ninth grade."

"Say what?"

"And I never ew! That was my first ew. And it was him. It was him. And I'm sorry! I'm sorry! I'm sorry! I'm sorry! I'm sorry! I'm sorry!"

"Hon-bun, here, here." She whisks Kleenex at me, and they are the extra-nice kind with lotion in them, and the ball of Kleenex—it's the kind of love I'd pay any price to receive.

And then, dropping to the floor, Daphne sets her two hands on my knees and prays.

"Dear sweet Jesus, please, Lord, heal Thea's heart, take this burden of pain and cleave her soul to her true purpose, the Mary Kay destiny you prepared for her way back in the womb."

By the time I leave, I've spent my entire paycheck, agreed to go to church, and signed a contract. In a week's time, I will be "pinned" in a ceremony—

Daphne's new girl, beautifying women, spreading the gospel of love via rouge.

And then … she comes back.

Not there one day, and there the next.

In the kitchen, making a pie, the summer plates neatly set around the table.

Hummingbirds and meadows.

A haircut, too. A retro, 1950s do, flipped out at the shoulders. New lipstick, cotton-candy pink. And something never before seen: an old-fashioned gingham apron with lace trim at the pockets. I will never forget the feel of it, pressed into her, holding onto her with all my might, sobbing, the lace imprinting on my cheek.

I do not say—*How could you?*

I do not say—*You hurt me!*

I only say—*Welcome back.*

Sprite. No spite.

The night of my pinning, I call Daphne.

"I can't do it."

"Sure, you can," she says. "You can do it, Thea! Know how I know? Because Jesus—he told me so."

I bite my lip. "I prayed last night, and Jesus told me *not* to do it."

"Thea, that's nerves talking, not Holy Spirit. From the moment I saw you, the Lord whispered in my ear, *That's her—that's your girl.*"

My heart about bursts. I'd do anything, wouldn't I? And I can see it: Daphne taking me under her perfumed wing, proudly pinning me, teaching me how to baptize women in Mary Kay and the Lord. Daphne, taking her rings off, one by one—a maternal foreplay.

"Can't you see it, Thea? You and me, driving off into the sunset in a pink Cadillac?"

I take a breath, dig in. "But the Lord said he doesn't want me selling makeup. He wants me selling burgers."

Her voice sharpens. "Well, I don't know why the Lord's telling us two different things. Do you?"

"No, I don't. I'm stupid about many things."

By September, the apron is gone.

(I won't know, until later, that Heathcliff is not a man. Heathcliff is a way of being in the world. Heathcliff can show up in the form of anyone at all. And what do you do? When Heathcliff arrives? When Heathcliff heaves antique cake stands at your head? It doesn't matter, in the end, if you understand why Heathcliff is Heathcliff. What matters is saying the hard word *abuse* in your head and believing it.)

There are many more hells ahead.

To witness and endure.

No boy will ever break my heart like she can.

Though it will hurt to remember Dane. Some mysteries never get solved. Yet, when I think of him, I will say, *Thank you.* It wasn't, after all, the outcome that mattered. It was the gift.

His gift to me much bigger—much graver—than a date.
The gift of knowing—*I could go.*
I could go with glass in my hair.
I could go while she watched and hated me.
I could go and tear those threads between us.
My own two feet were enough.
Foothills.
Wrinkles of mountains, made just right.
For walking away.

Kenton K. Yee

My God, It's Full of Astronomers

—After Lawrence Ferlinghetti

Amateur astronomers on August evenings
walking cats
in Aquatic Park
or carrying cockatoos
on their shoulders—
the cockatoos squawking about the drunks,
the drunks slapping at ants.
The amateur astronomers
spot Mars above a eucalyptus tree
and Venus behind cypress leaves
(but not the ants they're stepping on)
while a woman on a bench awakens
to the plash of the Milky Way
brighter than usual under the new moon
and swears at the Amtrak train
trumpeting the return from Reno
of one-armed-bandit victims.
It's near the hour
when amateur criminals come out for trouble
and amateur astronomers skedaddle home
to peer through amateur telescopes
for a closer look at one of the countless galaxies
of countless Earths waltzing among countless suns,
each Earth with countless parks,
each park (on average) with six ant colonies
and three amateur astronomers,
each one trying to see—
like the amateur ant astronomer on a leaf

pondering the possibility of ant life
beyond her colony
beneath the eucalyptus tree
behind the bench that rains crumbs
in Aquatic Park.

Leland Seese

in our twenties

torn between our torn black jeans
and colours by alexander julian
everyone we knew spectacular
or just about to be
digging mtv but surreptitiously
the medium so *déclassé*
smoking filterless gauloises
rive gauche wannabes
crowded knee-to-knee
cappucinos in cafes
we forward in this generation
with bob marley solidarity was
buying vinyl *sandinista!*
demitasses baudelaire and schnabel
sid vicious dead three years
talk and smoke and talk
and drink and fuck and talk
till one went off to harvard
another off to nowhere another
to a graveyard four others
music tour down the coast
mohawks fades and mullets
cornrows chucks doc martens
reeboks till the rumor spread
they made them in south africa
everywhere one summer
a poster plastered on abandoned
building walls words in cursive

we are the nineteen eighties
oracle for minds on sony walkman
rewind screaming every greening
generation's anthem: *we will change*
the world

Christopher Citro

Having Grown Inland I Can Make of Boats What I Wish

Inkwell Beach, Oak Bluffs

The extra splotch of darkness on the already-
night shore was me alone saying thank you
to the stones, the sea I seldom get to see
coming up then backing away. You'd think
it would tire, holding all those fins in its belly,
ships submerged with screaming, ships sunk
to create reefs, ships still ticking out there.
I know they're just trying to make money,
but when all I get are their lights in the distance
I'm able to reach out and pinch each electric bug,
pull it close, let it locate a spark inside me
to correspond. Leave these together to drift off,
remain alight. Look up at the stars. Someone
in a kitchen two streets in from shore is eating oranges
thinking dang I forgot how great oranges are.

Blair Lee

Colony

My sister was the only one who believed me when I said I heard the queen from a hive up in Michigan call me while I was picking cherries out in the country around Grand Traverse County. Jessie thought I was back on medication and getting "better," like my being able to understand the language of locusts, all singing together in the night, was a bad thing. It's not like I meant to hear them—it doesn't work that way—or that I even tried to listen to begin with.

But next thing I knew I was drawn to a bee farm just bordering the dunes of Lake Michigan. I brought my camper up to sleep with them and speak with them and learn from them. And I did. I learned a lot. They told me why they worked and died and reproduced. They told me we had it all wrong, the way of things. They asked why I licked at their vomit and buzzed unsettled when I said because it was sweet. One of the smaller male workers told me it would be like him drinking from my milk, would I like that? and—after cleaning the remaining honey from my fingers—I kept my hands to myself.

Problem was I got reported as a squatter, which the police also said I was, and said, too, to find somewhere else to go to or I could go with them, if I'd like. They gave my driver's license a good squint and asked *Anabelle Walker?* with a kind of laugh, then gave it back to me, as I'd likely need it to drive off *anywhere else* again. I thought of constant Jessie, always there, even through growing up, and everything with mother and her dying, and then the divorce, and even now. So I figured, since Jessie believed me before and since we were sisters, I'd go to her house. It seemed to make sense. After all, like I'd learned from the bees, we were a kind of colony.

She didn't answer when I knocked on the door, but I heard her whispering just inside. I said, Jessie, I can hear you, I can hear you through the window, you're loud, and the door swung open at me. I said you knew I was coming, I called on my way. But that was two months ago, she said, and she figured I'd be off somewhere else by now, maybe talking to loons. I'd never talked to a loon, but I told her I'm here now and wasn't she glad to see me? I was glad to see her—she was my sister. And she said yes and took me in and made me shower.

That night she had Molly and Milly get ready for bed early and sent them off to their separate rooms. I thought that must be nice, two girls like us and a big house like this. And what names! We didn't have names that went together like that, Molly and Milly, but I wish we had. Just Anabelle and Jessie. She said she'd sleep out in the living room with me, like how we did when we were little and Mom was alive. Jessie had a living room with a cathedral ceiling, so our voices echoed from one side to the other.

She handed me a pillow from the couch and asked if I planned on getting a job. I asked if she remembered the time Mom took us out to the Amish town in Indiana. When we were little. Remember back then? She said that she did, but really, have I been looking around? I said I have been looking around, where was Quincy? She said DC for business, and I figured so, typical drone behavior, and looked to Jessie's belly since it was fall. After all, maybe she'd heard the bees, too. Maybe that's why she believed me. She'd heard them and Quincy was cast aside for the winter, his singular task of mating complete. My sister said she'd been given a promotion in HR and maybe she'd see if there was something open for me in janitorial or mail. A promotion, I said, and cocooned myself in one of Mother's old throws. Congratulations. I told her I could believe that she'd been promoted, look at her house, with the granite and wraparound porch and stairs and all.

She asked if I planned to move on by Christmas.

Christmas? I said I don't know, it's soon, but I don't know. Did she want me to?

Jessie smiled at me, a sad smile, and got up then to check on Molly and Milly. I asked again if she wanted me to—to move on—because I could get a job. I couldn't imagine Jessie leaving me, too. Not Jessie. She said to make myself comfortable. I did and listened to her steps soften and fade as they moved farther towards the girls' rooms, a mother bee checking on her cells. I held my knees to my chest and listened hard, straining for that old, familiar sound. I wondered what she might say to the girls—if she would be plain and Jessie, or if she would whisper sweet night secrets like Mother had done for us—while the hairs on my body all stood up in an attempt to listen, the empty space of my ears pulling outward in an ache until they finally pressurized and then popped, the sounds all lost beyond me.

Megan Paslawski

My Own Private Villa Diodati

I didn't expect Tyler to invite me to his Byron-Shelley seance. He was a specific kind of queer—a second-year-of-grad-school queer, a queer who was always queering our heteronormative assumptions about his relationship with his wife. I was the type of queer who sucked a lot of dick. So far, our professors had found his skills more intelligible than mine, but I only felt resentful when I remembered the fellowship money I'd lost to Tyler. Mostly, I just wanted him so bad. I pushed my friends in the program—badly funded malcontents, dark whisperers of academic exploitation—to talk endlessly about him. "Do you think he's ever kissed a man?" I kept asking. "I mean, do you think he's ever pressed that lithe swimmer's body against some slutty little bookworm boy and cupped his face with those strong fingers?"

Finally my friend Danny took me out for coffee and said, "Look, I'm all for the gay thrill of a little anomie. You know how much I love Jean Genet. But your insistence on a limited and phallocentric understanding of identity is not a socially productive move." He was right, but I still wanted to know.

The seance invitation came at the end of our British Romanticism seminar, after Tyler had sparkled on the finer points of intertextuality and I had mumbled that William Blake was "a really weird daddy to claim." The night before I had cried at how beautiful Blake's watercolor angel men still looked after two hundred years, so I guess Wordsworth was wrong about emotion recalled in tranquility creating poetry. Then Tyler said something so good I forgot I was a lisping idiot. "Yes!" I cried. "That's the visionary aesthetic that pulses through his oeuvre." Our eyes met across the beige conference table. With great deliberation, Tyler wrote a few words on an index card and passed it to me: *1435 Sequoia Street, Apt. 3L. 8 p.m. tonight. A seance to raise Byron & the Shelleys.*

"Dress like Lord Byron," he whispered as we filed from the classroom.

The Tyler who greeted me that night had coaxed his hair into Percy Shelley's disheveled locks, and his open-neck shirt revealed a throat that could turn a man vampiric. "Beautiful," he said, fingering my velvet cloak. Its hour had arrived after years of hanging unworn in my closet. "I knew you'd do Byron right. Come see our Mary."

Somehow my Tyler fascination had never included a fantasy set in his apartment, but his living room still startled me. The only furniture was a daybed heaped with fur rugs; clusters of glowing candles illuminated the bare floor and walls. "Like an opium den by IKEA," I'd tell Danny tomorrow.

Mrs. Tyler—Caitlin—emerged from the kitchen in a loose white nightgown. She held a pitcher in both hands. I always thought of her as my rival, but Caitlin looked glad to see me. "Do you know how hard it is to get laudanum these days?" She handed the pitcher to Tyler, who set it on the floor. Caitlin gave me a lingering hug once freed. "We're making do with absinthe cocktails instead."

I tried not to squirm in Caitlin's embrace. Biking to the seance, I'd reviewed Tyler saying "dress like Lord Byron" and convinced myself I'd misunderstood his tone. We never read sexual subtext the same way in our seminar, so why would raising some old ghosts make monkish Tyler suddenly want my flesh and blood?

But both Tyler and Caitlin looked flushed and a little hungry tonight. They made a married-couple show of pouring me a cocktail and settling me between them on the daybed. The drink was awful, too strong and tasting of burnt rubber, but it erased my unease.

"So." With scholarly foresight, Tyler had prepared a keynote speech. "We're gathered here tonight in mutual purpose, with shared devotion to a transformative moment of literary creativity." Caitlin took my hand and squeezed it, and I squeezed back hoping it just meant we were best girlfriends. Tyler continued talking as if at a conference. Then he nudged my knee with his. "Mary, Percy, Lord Byron! We know your spirits still linger in every page we turn. Come visit us now and show us how to live in genius!"

My self-preservation skills, never good, had drowned at the bottom of my second cocktail. Whatever cult-lite vision Tyler was conjuring, I would join him there.

"We need to focus on them," Caitlin said. "On the Shelleys and Byron. We need to see them ...." She giggled tipsily, and I recognized it was cute. "We need to see them before we see them."

"Good idea." Tyler grasped my other hand and closed his eyes. When I imitated him, a memory from junior high surfaced. My English teacher had been a bow-tie firebrand who liked sharing the scandals our textbooks censored. "Oh yeah, Byron and Shelley looooved each other," he'd said one day. My classmates had laughed, but I'd seen Byron come down like the wolf on the fold to ravish Percy's sulky-rebel mouth. I had doomed myself to gayness forever as I imagined Percy reaching up Byron's Albanian dress.

Caitlin's body trembled beside mine. I wondered if she and Tyler had planned this seance for a long time, whispering things in the dark that Tyler never let surface in a classroom.

The window rattled loudly in its frame. "They're here," Tyler breathed, and he and Caitlin locked arms behind my back. They acted united, but how could they know they interpreted the Shelley-Byron triangle the same way? "Should we let them in?"

The ghosts waited for me to answer. We had a weird night ahead no matter what I said now, but I still wanted to impress Tyler and Caitlin with my reading skills even if my text was just the room. "Yeah, come on in," I said finally. "However you appear to us, we need you to appear."

Eliot Li

The Sock

Heather said she enjoys devirginizing nerdy freshman boys. She told me this lying next to me in my dorm room bed while plucking the hairs beneath my navel. Naked in the moonlight, she looked like a sort of pagan goddess.

I tried to stave off sleep because I liked this feeling, all the angst and loneliness gone, vanished. Poof! It's a state of mind I'll have trouble explaining to my future wife when she tells me she doesn't understand how you could ever sleep with anyone you don't love.

"Was that the right speed?" I asked.

Heather nodded, her golden hair making scratchy sounds against the pillow, her forearm covering her eyes.

She told me she'd been homeschooled by her parents in a remote redwood forest in Santa Cruz. Raised Wiccan, she'd celebrated Beltane by burning piles of sagewort in the hills behind their log cabin.

In calculus class, we boys were stiff, dried-out stalks of wheat, only half listening to our professor's lecture on integrals and derivatives, with Heather in the center of the room clicking her ten-colored pen. She swung her scythe right through us.

"It's amazing what some guys will randomly confess in the post-coital state," she said, running her fingertip across my forehead, as if she were painting calligraphy or casting a spell. "Did you know David has a sock that he uses to masturbate? He's kept the same one since 8th grade, red and white stripes at the ankle. He brought it with him to college, though it's lost its elasticity. He's never washed it, just puts it back in the drawer after he's done."

There were quite a few intimate personal memories I was getting ready to confide to Heather as I felt my heart opening up to the world. But then I reconsidered.

Years later, I run into David at a "Daddy and Me" music class in the attic of our local church. His son is a constant motion machine, even when the teacher isn't playing any music. He's crawling across the carpet, banging on other people's bongos, and David has to wrangle him back to his lap, his place in the circle. He calls his son Batman. I never learn the kid's real name.

My daughter Millie sits criss-cross applesauce on the floor, her tambourine resting on her knee.

After class, David tells me he's at Google X, works on one of their moonshot projects, some kind of contact lens that diabetics can wear, with technology embedded in it to monitor blood sugar.

I don't tell him that the whole time he's talking, I'm thinking about the sock.

"You remember Heather?" he says, his son tugging at his arm, pulling him toward their parked car. "I heard she sold her company for $100 million, exploited an unmet need in the medical billing industry. Some kind of Turbo Tax for physician practices."

"Oh, yeah?" I say, lifting my daughter and holding her against my chest. "Good for her."

On the drive home, in the rearview mirror, Millie's singing "I'm a Little Teapot." She's wrapped up in her car seat, wiggling her little toes. So cute. Makes the time spent in the class completely worth it.

The last time I'd seen David, we were playing air hockey in the Leverett House basement, junior year. He didn't grip the plastic air hockey paddle by the central nub, but rather just held the rim loosely with two curled fingers, shooting the puck forward with little flicks of his wrist. Neither of us were still seeing Heather, who'd gone on to earn Phi Beta Kappa in computer science. We were probably both thinking about her, though, as we slapped the puck between us.

At home, my wife's scraping the scales off a silver branzino fish she bought from H Mart. I sneak up behind her for a hug, and she drops the knife into the sink.

"Can I have a playdate with Batman?" Millie asks.

"Who's Batman?" my wife asks.

I think about how our two families might get together, maybe a picnic at Henry Cowell State Park in Santa Cruz, Millie and Batman digging in the dirt for banana slugs under the redwood groves.

Ross McMeekin

Theater

By this point, Professor N.V. Abenroth hated nearly every film he saw, but he had nothing else to do on this showery Saturday afternoon, so he walked beneath an umbrella from his one-bedroom apartment to the Royal Bay Theater to view an Ecuadorian film another professor—one he actually respected—had suggested. On the way he passed a new thrift clothing store—Coming Soon!—and dropped a couple dollars into the old mesh baseball cap of a beggar sitting outside. The beggar could have been handsome, except for the bister gap in his front teeth, one that could have been prevented by ten seconds of flossing every morning. The negligence annoyed N.V., so he tried not to think about it.

No one stood in line outside the theater, no surprise. N.V. took for granted that most people around there weren't sure of Ecuador's continent, much less its location on a map. He paid and passed through the thick black double doors into the lobby, basked in xanthic yellow light subdued further by clay-red carpeting and tan walls covered by movie posters. Soda: six dollars. Popcorn: more. He plodded up the stairs toward the showing and saw, on the far wall, a poster filled with the face of a famous male actor in a big-budget romantic comedy, a film he guessed the Royal only played to make up for the money lost by playing superior films from places like Ecuador. The famous actor had a near-perfect combination of features. N.V. thought of how a certain colleague might describe them in print: skin like rich, buttermilk frosting, fresh from the refrigerator; oil-slick eyes crowned with heavy-laden lids; a tough, neat nose, near celestial in form; thick, hickory eyebrows, threatening to escape; hair billowing and heaving, as if asthmatic, and so on. Odious.

N.V. been an unattractive baby, boy, youth, and then man, but he didn't recognize this until he was grandfatherly, as he was now—if only in age—with his face sagging like a mop draped over a bucket. He'd started in theater in high school, and in his youthful delusion he'd hoped to be a leading man, or if not a leading man, some kind of lead figure somewhere else, perhaps as a model in a magazine, or on a poster, in a window, recurring in people's minds like a catchy song, rather than what he actually was: a B-side that people never played. Still, he continued going to auditions while attending a private liberal arts college on the East Coast, where he studied films rather than star in them. There he learned to show no quarter to director or cast, and he was good at it, so good that soon his job was to help young people to pick apart films as a king might a portion of mediocre roast goose.

The credits played and he left. The Ecuadorian film was stale. The lead squinted through the entire film to portray intelligence, like a restaurant known for only one dish. But before N.V. could walk down the stairs to the lobby, he again caught sight of the poster of the stunning young actor in the big-budget romantic comedy, and the desire overcame him to possess it for a while. Maybe he could write a quick reflection for an online magazine about how it changed a person to have a rotten slice of pseudo-artistic capitalism's core on one's wall for a day or two. The theater had two copies, one rolled up in a packing tube, so he bought the second and walked back through the light drizzle to his apartment.

At home, he swallowed a benzo he'd saved from his prescription and chased it with syrah and laid out the poster on the kitchen linoleum, tamping its corners down with coffee mugs. He circled it, amused. The actor looked much different, there on the floor. Weak. Desperate. N.V. left the poster there and watched an old Meryl Streep film to clear his palate of the Ecuadorian failure while finishing the bottle of wine. As the credits rolled, he got up to make dinner. He stepped around the poster to the kitchen burners and sink and proceeded boiling the spaghetti too much. On a whim, he scooped a shod of limp noodles with the cooks fork and let it fall onto the actor's face with little slaps. He then took the small warming pot of Arrabbiata sauce and dripped some over those lovely eyes and mouth. There was a square of softening butter on the shelf, so he spread that with a knife over the star's neck and shoulders. It wasn't enough. He unbuckled his khakis and pissed all over it, the sound like rain on the hood of a car. Then, after watching the news for twenty minutes, he defecated on the poster. Afterwards, in the stench, he walked around the poster, feeling regnant. Then, careful not to drip anything on the floor, he curved the poster in on itself like a coffee filter around grounds and carried it down the steps outside to the dumpster, where he tossed it in.

He slept soundly until afternoon—it being a Sunday, he had no lectures to give—and decided he would visit the Royal and watch the film starring the stunning actor and write a scathing review, describing how its formula was based on a slew of constructs meant to sip the souls from the public, all to firm up the phalluses of the gentry. He walked from his apartment, sun flickering off the morning's rainfall, and half a block before the theater, he stopped short at the new thrift store, now open. There, he forgot the movie he was to attend, and forgot nearly everything else also, because in the front window, empty yesterday, was a mannequin so handsome a person might buy its clothes, just to resemble it. He swore, went inside, and bought the mannequin.

Jason Peck

The Juggernaut Enters the Ring

My garage used to be my sanctum, and now I can't stand it. Blame it on this new car I've got up on the jack, its undercarriage orange with rust, the paint color an ugly off-red like spoiled meat, mildew reek from the trunk filling my sacred space to the ceiling. A Ford Windstar, one of the best minivans for the all-American demolition derby. By now, I've transformed hundreds of cars like this into derby vehicles, driven them to the track and smashed them to scrap against the sides of my rivals. We should be in fighting shape, both me and the car. But, neither of us are there yet. Not even close.

Kathy's left me—up and gone midway through pulling the passenger-side window from the Windstar with a final *Fuck you, Kyle*. I don't remember too much else from that night other than kicking the windows to crystalline dust and passing out on the garage floor in a business-formal suit I haven't washed since. And yet, I can still imagine her in the garage with me, her translucent specter wearing the cream-colored blouse she wore like a uniform to her job managing student aid at our podunk community college. When she approached the ruined cars with a crowbar in hand, she brought to mind a receptionist who suddenly snapped. And me, I know what I look like. A stockbroker after the market crash. Halfway to homeless. Just given up.

A radio in the garage whispers Pantera on the lowest volume it can practically reach, but I winch my ears against the sound. The OxyContin makes my hearing sensitive. I earned myself a broken tailbone and two dozen stiches in my left arm at the Hooks County Derby last week, my only outing without her since high school. Since then, I've been keeping myself as immobile as possible. I'm squeezing out every second so my wounds can heal in time. Probably shouldn't be taking the meds with Molson.

Disassembly was Kathy's forte, not mine. If she were here right now, this car would already be in pieces, and I'd be sitting there and watching the brutal disassembly of a car—one of life's greatest pleasures, if you ask me. I know the window will pop when she attacks it then slide out once the cover is removed. The removal of the carpet will reveal the shining gray underbelly. The seats and door panels and dash, the molding and the door handles, will disassemble along their prefabricated lines. The windshield releases with the sound of suction; the bumper hits the ground with a clang that rattles the mason jars of screws and widgets in the garage. It's like watching Bob Ross on YouTube or a chef on the Food Network. I took comfort in the process—the inevitability of success at the end, the *certainty* of the execution, and at times she'd stare back at me with a look on her face that told me I was a little too absorbed.

I can build the monster by myself, is what I'm saying. But, I should have started. Kathy's not here to help. It's just me and the Ford, and why can't I focus on this car already? Why hesitate?

I blew it at the Hooks County Derby last week, plain and simple. I was taught that the worst cars smell like families: the moldy food, the poorly cleaned puke from a decade of flu seasons, the water-logged odor of clothes left rotting in the back. Too much of the everyday humdrum mileage that leaves nothing worth wrecking. And knowing that, I still strapped myself into a fortified Dodge Grand Caravan that made me gag a little, even after the bleaching.

But so what? I convinced myself. Plug your nose. Spritz the interior with Pine-Sol like a cheap cologne. The frame was solid, the battery worked. American cars are always best for derbies, hands down; that latent American machismo means steel frames versus cheap aluminum, an engine that roars. Enough horsepower, I figured, to compensate.

And I played it smart. I cruised the outskirts of the track, exposed less of my vehicle. I painted the car a middling tan color, so I was camouflaged by the dirt. When someone took a shot at me, I'd swerve in time and roll with the hit so good the blow barely scratched. Tires had churned the dirt track to mud and then down to something thicker, nastier, a soup that my car paddled through. The soil of war,

I'd always imagined—like the battlefield at Somme when artillery bombed the forest down to the mantle—and I waited again for that moment of awe to hit me, that out-of-body experience I always achieve despite the hundreds of times on the track, for that shred of disbelief that still stares wide-eyed and watches me doing something as loud and stupid and excessive as it gets. That's why this never gets old—it never gets totally familiar.

I backed to the edge of the track and accelerated forward with an angry sputter into an unsuspecting Hyundai with a bull's skull soldered to the hood. *I'm doing it,* I said to myself.

I sputtered to a modified three-point turn, cracked a Honda Odyssey in the passenger-side front, where the engine was already leaking black smoke, the first sign of impending vehicle death. Easy kill. "I'm doing this," I said out loud this time. Out of habit, I waved to the pit crew at the north side of the track, where Kathy would usually sit, and it hit me: No euphoria this time. No awe. The track was business, another item on my to-do list, along with getting my suit pressed and my sidewalk power-washed. At Hooksville, I operated off nothing but muscle memory.

Twenty minutes in, I was dodging around the cars who'd called it quits, waving to the losers and thinking to myself that I might actually have a victory at one of the sport's Big Twelve fairs. I felt more outside of myself than usual. But then, in the center of the ring, I saw a tricked-out Town & Country looking a little too passive and thought to myself: *Time for another scalp*.

A bad idea, keeping your attention in one place.

Out of the corner of my eye, I saw a flash of bumper coming so quick I couldn't even make out the model. I'd never dodge this one. And all I could think of—pathetic as it may be—was, *Why me?* This shouldn't happen to the prodigy who won the juniors at the West End Fair right out of high school, who placed at the Lowe's Motor Speedway in his third year of competition. Derby pioneer Larry Mendelsohn himself rose from his wheelchair, clapped me on the back, and said I was the future of the sport he had helped create. I'm Kyle Gardner, goddamned child prodigy, and the first rule of offense should be near-tattooed on the inside of my eyelids: Never forget you're someone else's target.

The only good thing about this feeling of helplessness is someone got it over with.

From what I discern later, an Escalade painted in the gaudy colors of a vintage roadster smashed into my passenger side with enough force to flip me, the kind of hit that makes the audience gasp while imagining the worst. Time slowed. The diesel engine's sputter made my eardrums ring, but I swear I could hear the trickle of gasoline from the fuel tank into the back seat. And then I passed out. No brave last stand at Hooksville. Just the buzzsaw vibrations as referees cut me out of the car, the aluminum taste of the dust from fire extinguishers hitting my mouth.

Mostly, I remember the silence, the crowd robbed of its adrenaline rush. Something they loved might have killed a man. In my imagination, some obnoxiously cute kid in the stands lost his dream of being a driver. *Mommy, Mommy!* he said through his gap-toothed mouth. *Is the man OK?*

Total buzzkill. The worst crime against my sport.

From the silence outside, I know it's late when I wake up on the couch where I passed out. Nothing, no whoosh of passing cars, no barking from the neighbors' Pekingese. Just the soft groans of the house itself as it constantly adjusts its weight.

I don't sleep in the bed anymore; I just pick the closest comfortable spot to collapse. Sleep isn't coming back; the beer lingers in my veins, keeps me wired. I don't bother checking the clock, just head straight for the garage, where the air is cooler.

I remove the passenger seat from the car and toss it to the floor without reverence. I peel the carpet, still plastered with crumbs and dust, and see the pristine interior bed. Next comes the display case, the dash, and I need to be careful not to clip any wires, but by the time I get that far, my hands are too numb. Fucking Oxy.

I call Kathy. It occurs to me well after the third ring that I've been too scared to call her lately. Any conversation with her these days feels like a virtual guarantee I'll say something stupid. I *am* doing something stupid: Upon further inspection, my phone says four in the morning. But, it suddenly feels like a far worse injustice that I haven't given this little Windstar the proper respect. The undercarriage is rusted, but shouldn't I care about what really matters? The engine that propels it forward? The imposing steel frame?

The phone keeps ringing, twice more now. The background photo assigned to Kathy blinks in tandem with the rings, that one picture where she's giving the peace sign in the foreground while the burning wreck of our Chevy Uplander at the 2018 Dayton County Derby lights up her face. *Pull me from the wreck later*, I told her, *but get the shot first.* The fact that I am calling my wife is an abstract thought to me until the phone stops ringing.

"That car we got before you left," I say. "The one that was out in the yard for two years under a tarp. I think we should name it."

Silence. In my haste, I assumed I was going to voicemail. But then finally, she speaks.

"You mean the one we got from the family going through a *divorce*?"

The word stings. Even though we're not there. Yet. "No," I say. "The Windstar that we found on Craigslist. I'm thinking we should name it something outrageous. Something over the top." I pause. "Like 'Ragnarök.'"

"Right. You see that thing and immediately think Norse apocalypse?" Her voice is an expert deadpan. "And you used that name already."

"What about 'The Ninja'?" I ask. The silence that follows is painful. I know I'm disappointing her again. "Probably good for sneak attacks."

"Clearly, you were looking at different axles." I hear her sigh through the phone, a long static whoosh. "Look. The Windstar was the worst of the 2000s-era vehicles. You drive the Windstar, you need to make it a tank. A battering ram. It's got no subtlety." Her tone is that of a salesman explaining Blue Book values to an especially stupid customer. "But why are you acting like you care? You haven't taken anything but your Wall Street job seriously."

"Wall Street?" I scratch my chin. "Babe, we live in Altoona."

"Whatever, Kyle. You wear a suit, you never call. And then you *do* call, and it's four in the morning."

"Are you derbying for someone else?" I say before I realize I have committed yet another separation faux pas. "'The Wrecking Crew'? Those clowns out of Scranton? I know you dated the driver in junior high."

"And you derbied without me at Hooksville." And then silence, not even static. She's hung up.

I think back to when I first met her on the family farm, with a line of derby frames circling the barn while her father, Jerry, taught me trade secrets. My memory's always fuzzy. In my imagination, she's Kathy in miniature, like a cartoon character with the adult head superimposed. Her look is '90s flannel meets blue-collar mechanic, heavy smudges of grease on her jean shorts. She could identify any car by make and model within seconds but only valued their ability to take a hit. "A BMW?" she said with a little smirk toward my parents' unworthy vehicle. "Look at it the wrong way and it smashes like a beer can."

Jerry rolled his eyes at his daughter. My father, hopelessly uncool, tried raising an eyebrow in mock amusement. Instead, it looked like his face malfunctioned. Maybe he realized then that this bizarre creature had claimed me for a life he would never understand.

The next day, in the acquisitions meeting, my neck is still killing me. My tailbone is definitely cracked, and the car door tore a gash along my forearm that took three-dozen stitches. I have a lingering worry of bleeding through my jacket sleeve. I'm alone in a conference room with my boss, Bob Gregory, and he's marking up some pie charts that look like pinwheels on the white board. I can't connect to anything we discussed the week before. And all the while, I'm sitting there with my pain and thinking to myself, *I deserve this agony. How. The.* Fuck. *Did I miss the fourth-place asshole that hit me?*

Bob Gregory knows something is wrong with me. I possess the telltale signs of a man losing his will to live—the absences Bob's been ignoring, the slow growth in the diameter of the bags under my eyes, my wrinkled suit where the stains are beginning to stand out. Of course, he assumes it's a bedroom issue. This isn't unusual for him. Despite being old enough to be my dad, he's also the guy who rediscovered his libido seven years ago, courtesy of four daily capsules of goat's weed. He wants to brag, but he he's also a devout Episcopalian. It occurs to me I never told him she left.

"Whoa," Bob says in that severely understated way he always does. "I'm sure she'll come back," Bob says after giving a sufficiently dramatic pause. "She seemed so nice."

"It's over, Bob. She said she didn't recognize me anymore."

He scrunches his face, raises a finger in alarm. A point has entered his head. It must leave through his mouth.

"You know what?" Bob Gregory says. "Pray on it. I know God will come through." He raises a hand before I can object. "No, I'm serious. Just pray."

"Bob …."

"Pray to whatever God you have. And don't report me to HR."

I've been neglecting my derby duties. Work commitments have been intruding these past few years. At our peak, a dozen per year, even back in the salad days, just out of college, when Kathy and I could barely afford the habit. Out of pity, Jerry would drop a car or two off at our apartment, a well-preserved piece he'd dismiss away with the obvious lie, "Total scrap. See if you can do anything with it." Now, our derby count is down to half that many. That old Ford still sits on the jack, and its bumper is looking like a frowny face that judges me.

So, it's inevitable I start getting haunted again.

In this dream, I'm walking through a derby field the night after the match. The wrecks haven't been cleared, the burnt-out frames still litter the ground. Cold moonlight reflects white off the empty bleachers. The scene's so clear that I stop to admire the handiwork of the fallen cars. A 2008 Toyota Sienna with a flaming eagle on the hood in acrylic paint. A Honda Odyssey with barbed wire wrapped around the middle where the trimming once was. A coal-black Hyundai Entourage with "Ragnarök" stenciled with gold paint in faux-runic script across the side.

Shit, I think—I did use that name already. All these cars were mine.

I keep walking. There's a muddy clearing in the middle of the field, and on cue, *whoosh*—an eruption of fire blinds me with angry red light. I shield my face with my forearm, smudge my face with my charred arm hairs. My eyeballs are dried to jerky. From the inferno, a giant comes into view, silhouette first—blazing fire breath, teeth like man-sized saw blades, tiny T. rex arms flailing up and down in jerky nutcracker motions.

Truckzilla. The traveling thirty-foot robot that chomps cars and breathes fire at derbies. Truckzilla, my avenging god, his voice almighty and all-capped, and here in my dreamscape, he's far more organic than the real-world automaton, his body come alive with sweaty realism. Here, the metal limbs ripple like muscle under the skin, and through the pipes that make his ribs I can see the engine expanding and contracting in time like a beating heart.

"ASSOCIATE VICE PRESIDENT OF OPERATIONS?" Truckzilla screeches in a voice of cascading fire and screeching steel.

I drop to my knees, prostrate. The smoke makes me cough. The moon has vanished; the only light is divine inferno. 'WHAT THE FUCK, KYLE? WHAT DOES THAT TITLE EVEN MEAN?"

"I don't know," I admit before adding, "Money. More money for derbying?"

"HAVE YOU GONE CIVILIZED?" Truckzilla bellows. "ARE YOU COMMITTED TO THE LIFE OF DESTRUCTION? OR DO YOU HAVE ANOTHER GOD BEFORE ME?"

Truckzilla turns his head to the sky and belches a column of fire that reaches higher than my eyes can follow. For all I know, the moon's a cinder, but I don't think he wants to fry me yet. This is a roar of disapproval. Of disappointment. *I put this much into you*, he's saying, *and what have you come to?*

Twelve years ago, this old Windstar in my garage was a glossy ad in a magazine, a thirty-second TV ad where it glided over a road that twisted like a giant tapeworm. I hope it had some good times before its final blaze of glory with me. But, I doubt it. A minivan sees more soccer practice and office commutes in the civilian life. It's the end of the derby season, and this is the only car I haven't transformed yet. And also—the only car I haven't wrecked.

The undercarriage of the Windstar is like the open mouth of a taxidermized animal. Everything else, all the little features and bells and whistles—the cup holder, the CD player, the power windows and airbags—mean nothing. Can't see them from here. All we have is the core—the horsepower, the frame. The things that really matter. But it has me thinking—what if I were up on that same jack like the car, exposed? Would my core be a savage? Or something lost to civilization?

I'm eating Chinese takeout in the garage when Kathy's brother Ted arrives. *This is it*, I think for a moment. *She made her brother serve the divorce papers.* But then I see the bundle under his arm, wrapped up in a quilt his mother sewed. That package clangs together when he walks up the three steps to the front door, and I realize I forgot the order I had placed with him for Windstar parts.

I'm still wearing the business-formal Hugo Boss suit I took to the office, and he gives me a once-over—the sight of me in the garage with anything other than the standard jeans-and-T-shirt garage-monkey combo is still something new. I offer him a kombucha I bought at Whole Foods—since his latest, so-far-successful release from rehab, Ted has been obsessive over his gut microbes.

"You got the goods?" I ask him a little conspiratorially. It's my attempt at a joke, but it falls flat. Always does. Our relationship has always been sparse on words, ever since we met when I was seventeen, and my attempts at bonding usually end in embarrassment ("So, you're an ex-con?" my pimply old self had asked. "Actually," Ted said, his voice level, "I'll always be an ex-con.").

"You know it, brother," he says. The familial callback deflates me a little. Brother-*in-law*, he means. For now. But then again, maybe I'm reading too much into his voice, jumping to the kind of conclusions that had the marriage counselor frustrated with me. Ted's always been like this, quiet and aggressively reserved, as though a moment of spontaneity would doom him. Given his background—*maybe* he's right?

I lead him to the garage. He doesn't ask to come into the house, and I'm grateful for that. Inside, the signs of desperation manifest themselves: the clothes laid haphazardly around the living room, the coffee table now almost covered in beer bottles, the heavy smell of the cigarette habit I've picked up, the fine layer of crust developing on the dishes in the sink. Like an amoeba, the disorder stretches and tests its boundaries, and its corners are reaching the doors of my garage. So far, I've managed to find enough motivation to keep it spotless. But, the mess, I know, is patient.

At the workbench, he carefully unwraps the package. There are six of them: heaters—exhaust pipes that will extend from the hood of my car to keep the temperature off the engine. Like six walrus tusks, six horns from the head of a demon beast. They serve a purpose, but honestly? Any driver will admit they just like the noise. That angry sputter of an unfiltered engine, a roar so powerful it shakes you down to the spine. It's the last step in assembling a derby car—the final finishing touch. Ted's confusion is palatable when he sees I've barely started taking it apart, let alone putting it back together. Still remaining: disassembling the car, soldering the door shut, reinforcing the bumper, padding the inside, relocating the engine and fuel tank, adding Ted's contribution. Everything, basically.

"I still have to take this thing down to the frame." I take a sip of beer and gather my thoughts. "I got a few leftover cage bars I can use.

The axles are in great shape. I'm going to get a lot of mobility out of this one." Ted takes a look over at the naked undercarriage and frowns. One look and he sees through my bullshit.

It's silent for a few moments, awkward. Ted coughs into the kombucha, shifts his feet on the concrete floor and fills the garage with his shuffling. He looks back at the car then to the shelves of tools. I can see the scales in his brain weighing his family loyalties.

"She's fine," he says before I can ask.

"Did she say anything about me?" I ask, because I know Ted has undoubtedly visited Lancaster in the immediate past, where Kathy's staying with her mother. Has she given any thought to ending the cold war here? Give me something, Ted. Do a favor for the guy who drove you two hours from Cleveland to Pittsburgh, with you shivering in the back seat during your 2012 relapse. Give me something other than, "She's fine."

Ted gives me a look that I interpret as inner turmoil. I walk over to the workbench where I left the headers and examine them. Clean-cut steel with the complimentary mirror polish, even though the competition will crush them flat. Soon, Ted will leave, and I'll be alone in this garage to disassemble again—just a crowbar and a screwdriver and a head full of half-formed motivations that I probably won't act on.

Say anything but fine, *Ted. Please don't give me a goddamned generality.*

"She's fine," Ted repeats, and I nod and pretend I have found something incredibly interesting in the pipe beyond my own face squashed to toothpick-thinness in the funhouse-mirror reflection. I hear Ted running his hand on the underside of the car. For the first time, he seems to notice the old picture of Jerry in the back of the garage, the one from the '60s, in which his dad wore the fluffed bomber jacket to imitate a flying ace. He gives our mentor a quick two-finger salute. "At least it's got no family smell," he says of the Windstar.

At any given point, there's a half-dozen people across this country that make a living from this—like *really* make a living. Quit their jobs and tour the country, practice maneuvers eight hours a day. At fairs, they sign autographs—Alan Arnold, the Glass Face, who broke his nose so many times on the steering wheel it turned Z-shaped; Martin Vee, the Flying Dutchman, who went airborne over bumps in the turf; Rosie Fitzwilliam, who retired from driving school buses to wreck them in the super-heavy division. The rest of us make do. We sneak in precious minutes in between our jobs and families, squirrel away the savings on equipment and cars the elite throw out.

I was going to make a career of this. Jerry himself said so.

Jerry's secret? He bought cars *after* the derby finished them, and he taught me to recycle the cages and the brackets, the power hoses and bumpers. From the cars that survived multiple runs, I learned how they reinforced the frames, which models fought hardest, where drivers put their switches and emergency fire extinguishers. Drivers and cars are both the same—to learn, just see what's broken the next day.

I started wearing a neck brace like a giant donut from the first time I heard something crack. I started wearing steel-toed boots after watching someone get his leg caught between the transmission and the floor. There's a spot on the dashboard where a hit from behind drove my fist into the dash and broke three fingers, a back bar where I cracked my elbow. *There*, you think to yourself in the emergency room, *that would have been a great place for some extra padding.* Seat belt versus harness? How much mobility will you sacrifice for safety?

I used to love the hurts the next day, feeling my injuries healing themselves into scars that wouldn't be hurt the same way twice. I was evolving into something meaner, tougher. Ten years of this, and I hit the majors. At Altamont, my name appeared on the bill as a supporting act to the headliner. That poster's framed in my garage, along with the dozen or so trophies I collected, the ceremonial plaques that look like championship belts.

"Trust me," Jerry said. His cancer diagnosis was three years away by then. The Viking funeral we held in the back of a flaming Mustang only two years away. "You have this. Sure as I've been of anything in my life. Keep going and you got it."

And I *went*, man—kept cutting through my opponents with nerves shot full of adrenaline, so happy I let out a whoop every time I scored a hit. Every time I *got* hit. Every time I just got behind the wheel of the vehicle, period. And then one day I stopped.

Bob Gregory makes me the formal offer for the assistant vice president spot after the clients have left out lunch meeting. It's getting to early evening, and the happy-hour crowd is filtering in. They've got the lights turned low. They're aiming for ambiance, maybe. To me, it's just dark. The drinks should be fancy, too, but I'm downing them way too quickly, and I'm explaining to him how I can manage the next derby despite my injury because I once drove through a side door splintering in my stomach. Bob Gregory turns to me and says something like, "You just drank cabernet and ate bluefish pate back there with our clients."

I blink. I'm a bit foggy with Scotch, but I watched him schmooze three clients into ten-year extensions. I know what he's pulling here. He's changing the subject to something I know I should see coming but can't totally understand. All I can do is raise an eyebrow and play along.

"I'm saying you're maybe more suited for Freshwater Capital than you let on," he says. "All this talk about breaking your hand against the steering wheel—I just think you're letting your hobby get in the way."

"I like wrecking cars."

"I like exercise. But, I'd lose interest if I'd been doing it for years and it hadn't worked out for me."

Ouch. How dare he challenge my devotion to the passion I've had since before I could drive? And fuck him and his grandfatherly way of speaking, which disarms me into silence. I want to explain to him how it's about loving the same thing that amazed me as a child. Did I, as a child, ever dream about leading an all-hands meeting about expanding the Seattle branch? Did Bob Gregory?

Probably. I suspect that's his problem.

"I don't think I'm cut out for a vice-president spot."

"You keep saying that. And yet … you close these deals. People trust you because you're not me. You came from outside the company."

The silence that follows feels rehearsed, almost. Both parties have agreed to silent contemplation. I sip my Scotch. Bob Gregory's eyes pass lightly over the barmaid's ass as he orders another drink.

"But I don't really love what I'm doing," I say. "At Freshwater, I mean. No offense or anything."

"I never loved it, either," Bob says, and right then I would love to imagine that there's some kind of sadness on his face, some kind of regret that he never stuck around to pursue some passion he had. *This is all there is.* But, there's nothing there—just the quiet acceptance. "This job," he says, "it just paid the bills. Nothing else."

☾

I come home drunk and smack my arm against the wall until it feels like a stitch has popped. Kathy is gone, and I want to hurt. I want to embrace the pain because it's something Bob Gregory would never do. Because I didn't say no to the offer, just sat there with a forced little smile that he took as acceptance.

The plan has gone awry. This job at Freshwater—it was supposed to be a means toward an end. After years of working in a garage, we decided we'd make a few sacrifices to keep the dream going. I'd get a real job, make use of my obligatory bachelor's in finance. We called in favors from my father, who never approved of Kathy or derbying but knew people from Freshwater. I started answering phones. Customers would complain about their escrow balances, and I'd smile through a grin so forced my teeth hurt and daydream about smashing their Mercedes-Benzes in half with a perfect jackknife. But, money made a difference. Money bought the house with the four-car garage, the free time to prowl for derby cars. That first year at Freshwater, I won the Dakota Badlands Derby, then stood on the podium at Altamont with an oversized bottle of cheap champagne I was meant to spray over the other drivers. Instead, we took it home and got drunk, turned the music up loud enough to shake the garage, and then we fucked—awkwardly, carefully—in the ruined backseat of our award-winning wreck. As close to a perfect day as it gets, and we were due for a hell of a lot more of them.

Now, here I am, ten years later, and the knife-edge balance between my lives is off, bent forcefully in the direction of Bob Gregory and Freshwater Capital. I developed a taste for twelve-year-old whiskey. I learned golf. I stopped escaping, settled for existing. And when it came time to plan out the derby season, the excuses came from me. Little moments built. Barbs back and forth over the changes that were happening in our lives. I remember talking about comfort. *But how are we happy?* she asked back.

I start thinking of when I lost her, and I can't. There's no blowout moment. The exact tipping point escapes me, but as I drink beer after beer and feel myself propelling toward a hangover that's going to hurt, the point comes into focus: I grew annoying, boringly old. And I think about calling Kathy tonight after all and making some big grandiose plans: *Take me back*, I'll say, *and I promise I'll be good*. I'll take this Windstar and turn it into my best car yet. I'll name it something outrageous and paint its moniker on the side so everyone knows to take a shot at it. *The Enforcer?* No. *The Commander?* No. *The Juggernaut!* I'll name my car *The Juggernaut*, and I'll paint this thing bright yellow and dare the rest of derbydom to try me, because I'm Kyle fucking Gardner, heir to a pedigree of champions, and any other punk-ass driver is going to need a sixteen-wheeler to stop me.

There's a lot more ranting to make, and as I drink, I have the impression that little of it is internal. Is my voice echoing off the garage walls back to me? Sleep comes sloppy and sudden, as it always does these days.

The dream's so real, the smoke makes me eyes water. The empty lot of demolished cars, the volcano eruption of flame, and then Truckzilla emerging from the smoke, Disney-villain style. Is he bored of me by now, of his constant demands that I pay tribute? Hard to read a face made of steel.

"YOU SMELL OF COMFORT," Truckzilla says. "COMFORT AND OVERPRICED SCOTCH."

Enough, I think. *The fuck is he to talk to me like that?* I cross my arms. Truckzilla pauses.

"Let's make a deal," I say. "Let's say I quit my job at Freshwater Capital."

"NO DEALS. NO GUARANTEES."

I can feel the ground rumbling. But this time, God doesn't scare me. This time, I stare straight ahead when he turns his nose to the sky for his breath of fire, and I keep it on him when he turns his attention downward to incinerate me down to the skeleton. But, nothing happens. There's a gust of wind like a candle going out. The fire vanishes from Truckzilla's mouth. The sky changes back to the cold blue light of the moon. Dew condenses on the hoods of the ruined cars; a fire had never burned.

"As I was saying …," my voice echoes, "… here's what I plan to do."

As I speak, the ruined cars around me begin to fade. There's something new coming into view, the Windstar in my garage transforming layer by layer, its ugly paint peeling off in sheets, its windows cracking and exploding from view, orange welding lights sealing the doors shut while the heaters emerge from the hood with a groan like the transformation of a werewolf—something so beautiful and deadly it makes me cry, and I think to myself, This is *it*. My juggernaut. My last chance, and then onto the next last chance.

"Here's what I plan to do," I say to God, and this time, God listens.

Benjamin Davis

The Fourth of July for Beginners

The Fourth of July is a day where people celebrate killing a bunch of other people (killing is when you make someone die [to die is to not wake up (to wake up is to open your eyes)]). On this day, I am on an island you need a boat to get to (boats are things like cars [cars are things people use to get around and sometimes kill people (see: to die)]). A parade (big fun queue that goes nowhere) runs through town and everyone cheers for America (a piece of land with lots of people called a country [not to be confused with "Earth"]). Kids play soccer (kickball) and baseball (hit ball) and eat hot dogs (you don't want to know) with sun-warmed chips (thin potato things that have a lot of salt [fun fact: the people we are celebrating killing call french fries "chips" (we call french fries "french fries"). It is for all of these reasons that adults [large children with nobody to tell them no] play a game called war [you wouldn't believe me if I told you about war]) and by the end of the day, everyone is pleasantly exhausted so they go home to sleep it all off.

Kevin Carollo

Lease Help

What will your eyes say?
–Sappho

I heard it on the new conduit:
a refugee camp on the island
of Lesbos with a capacity of

three thousand currently has
19,400 residents. One of them,
an unnamed eight-year-old girl,

died in a fire last week. There are
no more words to say it, Marie.
There is no more legroom in

my brain for irony. When I said
eighty-five residents of Paradise
died in the fire, I meant it literally.

Yet I find my catgut tongue
poised to pay lip service to
the idea of thousands more

dying overnight. Dear Future,
let me get this right. Let me be
like the Yeti, or at least the ghost

of a crow of a big idea flitting
from door to door. Release
my small head from fake news

headlines: Mood ring factory
files for bankruptcy. Rabbit's
foot industry begs for bailout.

When I opined any incoming
universe can become a basic
totem or spiral out of control,

I meant it elementally. So how
many birds per minute can you
Skype? What if I told you they

absolutely positively had to be
in Lesbos overnight? O bless
the many creatures, big and small,

still open for pickup or delivery.
I'll be counting wild amoebae
until you see fit to get back to me.

Kevin Carollo

Goat's Head Soup

7:21a.m. and no sign of light At the Comfort Suites in Benton
Harbor Michigan at the tail end of 20— I woke up three
nights straight at 7:09 a.m. Everything seems to be about timing

Now I'm back in Dakota trying not to hurt the poetry I'm
wondering if 20— is a prime number It is now 7:26 a.m. and
no sign of natural light I should have been more specific about

meaning I should have mentioned the streetlight and how its
pale orange glow reminds me of an alien eye as per *The Day*
the Earth Stood Still A phrase like "pale orange glow" hurts

the poetry This is another day the Earth stands still It is 7:30 a.m.
and I'm wondering about dying at the end and how to go about it
and if this is just one more thing we should've planned better for

Everything seems to be about being alert and spoiling 7:37 a.m.
and the snow on the roof of the Monet haystack that is the house
across the street seems suffused with a dark yet distinct shade of blue

That house was sold one summer for $124,800 or thereabouts after
just four days on the market I think about how we, like it, are statistical
anomalies "Suffused with" hurts the poetry whereas "when all is said

and done" is an interesting turn of phrase as is "turn of phrase" come
to think of it It is way more interesting if there is something after
dying at the end It is 8:08 a.m. and I've been distracted with making

coffee and now watching what might eventually turn into snow
Poetry about winter and snow and cold in general hurt the poetry
I thought after all this running I'd no longer be afraid to go outside

I promised myself a gander at a gaggle of wild turkeys on a day
with a high of twenty-eight I have to feel like I'm taking my life
in my own hands When I think about a phrase like "it makes you

wonder" and how it doesn't aurally rhyme with "over yonder"—
another curious phrase—it's like refiguring the literal and natural
order of things I don't know what I've done with the morning I've

been on the phone with my mom discussing my brother who
suffers from bipolar disorder My bro's husband called my mom at
5:30 a.m. Eastern Standard Time and no sign of light Sometimes at the

westernmost end of that time zone there is no light until 8:30 a.m.
After four months or so of mania my bro has finally crashed and
will go back to Four Winds in upstate New York at 2 p.m. EST on

January 7, 20— which is today Confessional references to one's
family members in real time in a poem must both violate a kind
of privacy and hurt the poetry I'd planned on calling this poem

"Nocturnal Aubade" I was just using the file "Goat's Head Soup"
because there was nothing much inside it and I thought I should
maybe make use of all that dead white space I'd opened up a year

or so ago I'm listening to Madonna in the hopes that it will save
my bro I once quoted Madonna to my bro over the phone when
she was feeling down I told her "Never forget who you are little

star" *Ray of Light* is actually a very good record Maybe if I keep
still as a deer might on a lake with too-thin ice I can find a way
to fill in the proverbial blanks I'd like to think that 20— will be

a better year than 20— was, but you, ray of light, know as well
as I do that people in power and/or the forces that be want more
of the same just as there were 504 murders in Chicago last year

and by January 2nd of this one there were already three more I'm
trying to convince myself that power emanates from everywhere
and that true revolution is when we take our lives into our own

hands Bataille might say that power is when the sun shines out
of our anuses and I have to confess that at the edge of my seat
this makes a strange kind of sense to me I'm willing to entertain

the idea of rosaries turning to gold in the Balkans in the hands
of Catholics who believe Madonna appeared to several locals
on a hill for several nights straight And on the third night they

made goat's head soup The phrase IN GOD WE TRUST was not
printed on American money until 1956 Factoids anecdotal
evidence and newspaper references in poetry hurt the poetry

I always fail to understand what happens to the morning or why
the way you break a line of poetry can make or break the poem
I'm failing at keeping up with what's happening to the world

outside I'm keeping quite still on the thin ice of my anus from
which all sweetness and light is emanating On Earth as it is in
Heaven I'm a still life waiting for a piece of snail mail I feel like

Goat's Head Soup the album 10:19 a.m. and time to do something else
Reading other people's poetry no doubt hurts the poetry Ordering
something online must be like making a pact with the devil No poetry

but in wings I call no dying or dying trying without first making sure
we're all all the way to the very end As for hurting the poetry to spite
ourselves again and again there is no telling there is no telling

Laura Lee Washburn

Remedy

What broke my mother's skin
so she bled without stopping?
What broke my mother's skin
so they had to stop her bleeding?

Not the thorn of a pencil point.
That resides in her left arm, blue dot,
reminder of school and boys.

Not the bicycle her mother
wouldn't let her ride, the skates
she couldn't try. Not the beach
where she couldn't swim. No.

What broke the skin over her shin
so two decades later she was blue still
where they stuffed the wound
with kitchen stove soot? I remember
the blue. I remember the soot.

What she wants is the missing tooth,
the straight toe, the unbent
trigger finger. She learned
not to smile wider, to wear
contact lenses, never to drape a scarf.

I frighten doctors
with the white scar over my wrist

where the bedframe fell. For
a few weeks I stared at
the doctor's two pin-mark dots
in my right-hand grip
but only until the coins
no longer fell through my not-closed fist.

A man drags his leg. A man
uses his wrists to move his new wheelchair. The child lives
in the hospital crib. The heart races
too fast into the world. Her blue
shin is reminder, her blued skin, remedy.

Laurie Marshall

The Geology of Grief

Carrie wakes from a sweat-soaked dream with her throat tight and dry like she'd been eating chalk. For the third time this month, tonight's dream featured a small man, no bigger than her son Joshua's superhero action figures, standing on her chest. Despite his diminutive stature, the man's weight threatened to crush her rib cage.

Every time, the dream plays out the same way: As she suffocates in her bed, she is panicked by the thought of her son finding her dead body. She attempts to fill her lungs, but her dusty trachea objects.

In her dream, Joshua is frustrated by the request from the funeral home to choose clothing and makeup for their staff to use as they preparc her body for the service. He dumps all the makeup in her bathroom drawer into one of the dozens of gift bags Carrie saved in the hall closet. In her dream, he chooses a bag from his twelfth birthday—the one with an image of Captain America's patriotic shield and a banner that reads "Happy Birthday, Hero!" At the funeral Joshua realizes his mistake, as the shadows and lip color he provided have turned his mother into someone unrecognizable.

One of the things Joshua doesn't know about his mother is that she buys makeup because it represents hope.

One of the things Joshua doesn't know about his mother is that like his favorite superheroes, her insides don't match her outsides.

Carrie sits at a small table in the predawn light near her kitchen window and waits for her eggs to boil. On the table, she turns and smooths the pages in a book about rocks and minerals she gave Joshua for his fifteenth birthday, the year he asked for a rock tumbler. She studies each illustration, tracing the edges of the 2D stones with her finger. She imagines texture where there is only smooth paper and colored inks. She imagines paper cuts where there are only loops and whorls.

The book says some minerals can grow into empty spaces and form rocks called geodes. Where there is plenty of room to grow, crystals are fully formed. These geodes are prized by collectors. If there is too much mineral or not enough space, the crystalline structure becomes solid and indistinct. The material grows until there is nothing left to distinguish the crystal from the rough rock material around it. The book says you can tell which geode contains the more desirable interior based on its weight. A heavy stone is full of solid mass and has lost its beauty. Its value is diminished.

A kitchen timer dings to say the eggs are done. Carrie pours the boiling water down the drain and replaces it with cold.

It's been eight months since Joshua's death, but Carrie's chest still feels heavy, even after she wakes. Despite the meditation and the grief therapy and the CBD oil, she dreams often of the little man, but tonight, she dreams she is eating stones. She holds each one in her mouth, resisting the urge to swallow, but panics as her body begins to float off the ground. Each time she begins to drift upward, she clamps her teeth together around the stone, gulps, and settles back to Earth. Undesirable geodes fill the empty spaces in her substrate.

When morning finally comes, she throws her soaked T-shirt and clammy bed linens in the washer for the fourth time this week.

Carrie lights the flame under a small pot of water and two eggs, dials the kitchen timer to ten minutes, and sits down to wait for sunlight.

Aimee Parkison

The Story of Jane

Collaged in shallow sculpts, real hair tacks into photographs of hair, lipstick applied to photographs of lips. In paintings of faces the size of women's faces, Jane wears vintage jewelry pierced through paper ears. Sketched faces, makeup applied to paper, powder, liquid eyeliner, mascaras scrawl on pages. Shellacked eyes hold gaudy eyelashes stroked by fingertips. Glued eyelashes curl from the pages as if from real eyes.

My eyelashes tickle the boy.

He shudders when he touches my pages.

The first time it happened, I didn't mean for my eyelashes to charm him. I was in the book with Jane. He was examining me along with other women, gazing into our mouths like vents, holes in holograms nestled inside the repurposed pizza box. The oily cardboard reeked of oregano. My mouth was scented with marinara sauce, whispering of fresh tomato, the velvet texture of olive oil.

My areolas smelled of old parmesan.

Blooming from busted fake-wood paneling, flowers with women's names were as tall as people. The boy never understood why the flowers were wonderful and yet worrying, never told his mother the photographed women inside the book looked like she did.

As he turned the pages through the screaming, through the shouting coming from the blood binding, he wanted to understand the story of Jane, the woman on the first pages, dragged out of her house and into the van with string to bind her hands before fingernails began scratching DNA evidence into her face.

He turned the brittle stained scratch-and-sniff pages smelling of decay with a sweet undertone that reminded him of chocolate. Other pages smelled of fear, blood, vomit, bleach, urine, and burning.

Where my dear Jane walked alone, her screams smelled of the night wind, exhaust from an old pipe, gasoline, and cigarettes. The boy leaned into my gaping mouth, scratched the page, and sniffed to inhale August sunlight on oaks and wild mint growing in ravines where I had wandered.

My face found its way into the Book of Screams several years ago. After Jane tried to save me, I was in the hospital for six weeks before I realized something had gone wrong. I couldn't believe what I was seeing. "Don't come near me!" I said to the boy, though he didn't hear.

Even now, I dream my body back, gridlocked in the death tunnel beneath the house on the hill. Here the vile odor of life cut short permeates elegant women like Jane, her hair styled in blood.

The dead, I understood their faces. I've scheduled multiple funerals this year, including my own.

When fear is a gift, Jane emerges from the dark house to fight for me.

Jane gets into the car with me and the crying girl, her handcuffed wrists straining.

Having fought for me, Jane no longer emerges from the dark house because the dark house emerges in the light where I see my best friend in the fireplace.

The victims' families face the photographic evidence with press releases about the way we disappear only to appear in the Book of Screams incriminating someone's husband, someone's father.

The book is bound with blood glue, pages of pressed and stretched dried skin, threaded with hair. The book smells putrid and sweet, but the boy doesn't want to talk about the smell because I've told him what it means. He loves the book too much. It's the kind of love that will make him a good cop or a successful murderer.

He sniffs the book secretly, not wanting his mother to know. He inhales deeply, huffing dried blood, old hair, perfume, and tissue. He sniffs bloody faces, fissures, inhaling the air inside the sockets of my gouged-out eyes.

Our families study the stars at night, knowing we are all love stories, but in some love stories things happen that have nothing to do with love. Sometimes, through no fault of their own, love stories become the walls of condemned houses painted with clusters of flowers of women's names.

One of the flowers has my name, the purple iris, weeks before the demolition so that the city tears down painted flowers, not blood-stained walls.

Search the entire room for Natalie, and there are no signs she is there, behind the paint, under the floorboards with me. If you see us in deep flowers like shadows, part of the underground artists' big picture machine, the petals make you mine: the pink, yellow, orange, purple, violet, magenta, red, blue, green, toxic neon, and white.

The woman in black lace cartwheeling over my unmarked grave, another aspiring singer, haunts the magnificent Art Deco Theater condemned in Los Angeles. Men who make films about us call themselves underground artists for stealing unclaimed corpses of murdered women to make snuff films in reverse.

Out of their underground movies, a new Hollywood—born of desiccated, desecrated remains—reanimates the dead through makeup, CGI, and lighting.

Broken bodies untangle, hydrated, breathing.

The captured walk free with unmurdered women rewound to life.

I walk backward on rewind with women and girls I love.

Jane is with us; so is Natalie.

Second chances play in reverse. Our end is beginning.

My long-brittle corpse recomposes into a daughter dancing.

Meghan Phillips

In the Town Where the Final Girl Lives (Interlude)

Donna: Every horror movie has a final girl.
Brooke: Final girl?
Donna: The one who survives it all and lives to tell the tale.
—American Horror Story: 1984

There are hunting accidents. A gun misfires. A guy nods off in his deer blind and rolls off the edge.

There are farm accidents. Someone gets kicked in the head by a cow. Someone falls off a horse. Someone gets their sleeve caught in a thresher. Someone drowns in the corn silo.

In the town where the final girl lives, there are suicides and overdoses. Domestic incidents.

About twenty years ago, a kid broke into his friend's house and shot his friend's parents, his little sister. Shot them dead in their beds. The friend wasn't even home. He was sleeping over at some other kid's house.

About twelve years ago, a twenty-year-old killed his fifteen-year-old girlfriend's mom and stepdad. They made it to Kansas before the cops caught them. News crews in helicopters trailed them down the flat of the highway. Everyone watched the pursuit on CNN.

In the town where the final girl lives, there are car accidents. The same year the football team won the state championship, five of the teams' seniors rolled a ragtop Jeep out by the Laser Dome. None of them were wearing seatbelts. There's a memorial to a girl who died when her car slid of the road and hit a telephone pole. When she got out to check the damage, a snapped cable lashed down and broke her neck.

The point is: There have been other tragedies in the town where the final girl lives. They already know how to grieve. They have had plenty of practice.

Julia LoFaso

Baby School

"The baby's mouth should be over the nipple like it's a sandwich," the lactation consultant says as she positions the rubber mouth of a baby doll over a cloth model of a breast, "like it's a hamburger."

The horror, I think, of being frozen open-mouthed like this baby, constantly rooting for a breast that only appears during this class. The horror of being me, a hamburger.

It took me fifteen minutes to walk two doors down the hospital hallway to milk class. Nurses with their rolling carts blew by me at impossible speeds. The first problem is the dead weight in my legs and feet, swollen to three times their size from fluids administered post-surgery. But the bigger problem is the pain that thunders through my abdomen intermittently. It's sudden and unpredictable, pain so fierce it trains me instantly. Guarding against it, I shuffle, inch. I do everything I can to not anger it, still uncertain which moves are the wrong ones. I laughed, yesterday, and I won't make that mistake again.

To prepare for this class, I slowly zip a hoodie over my softest of soft gray T-shirts, the only one my freshly excavated body can handle touching. I feel vaguely fancy about the addition of this hoodie until I reach the classroom, where other new mothers wear plush robes and silk kimonos, presumably brought in by partners or packed in advance, in a former lifetime. But I'm also newly aware that I'm an animal, that we all are, which allows me access to the unfamiliar sensation of not giving a fuck what I look like.

I am in awe of myself just for making it here, notebook in hand, ready to absorb facts into a new brain that feels like a dark landscape seen from space, dotted with wildfires. I haven't yet read the studies suggesting that the release of oxytocin hormones in childbirth may make the mind more pliable, may unlock something, but I do know that since my daughter was born my memory has been in a state of avalanche, dropping pebbles of random knowledge I haven't thought about in years. Since yesterday, I have had on loop in my head an imperfectly rhymed set of lines from a Babysitter's Club book I read at age nine or ten and the chorus of "Say You'll Be There" by the Spice Girls, a song I've never liked and didn't realize I knew every single word to. I have faith that my reactivated memory can only increase in profundity from here.

I am mildly excited to be at this version of school. Baby school. I am here and my baby is in the nursery. It isn't yet strange to be away from her. Independence is still my normal state.

The lactation consultant is maybe fifty or so and has a short, windswept haircut. Scrubs and a cardigan blur the shape of her body, and she reminds me of any number of my elementary school teachers.

I am alone at this class, but most of the other new mothers aren't. The partners are all men today: They minister to the mothers with little micro-movements—swooping for a dropped blanket, setting up a snack and water bottle station—and write down everything said in the class with the focus of calculus students, as if a baby were a code to be cracked. I'm not wishing, at this moment, for my partner to be here. I'm thinking, instead, in whatever altered state I've entered, that all these little movements—while technically quite considerate—seem superfluous, ridiculous, a show put on to shield us from our animal realness.

The laptops. The three-part questions about schedule, technique. How, I wonder, are these new fathers maintaining the illusion, after what we've just been through, that anyone is in control of anything, that the contentment of an animal that sprung from another animal can possibly be bought with the proper brand of breastfeeding pillow? I tell myself they haven't lived through our loosening of ligaments, haven't physically embodied the dissolution of the man-made world.

This early in my mothering career, coasting on a cocktail of love hormones and Percocet, I feel so psychedelically wise, so fucking cool with it all. The anxious Internet dives into infant napping protocol and sleep training theory, the obsessive measuring of pumped milk: All this will come later. But two days in—this ruled by the caprices of my deflated body, this close to feeling as if I've choked on a salty mouthful of the infinite universe before thrashing to the surface to cough it out in the form of a child—I am not yet prone to overanalyzing.

Which isn't to say that I'm not deeply naive: On day two of motherhood I still expect things to make sense, for facts to be facts. But the facts from this class, the facts we write down with varying degrees of focus, will be contradicted by facts from a second class I will take tomorrow, as well as visits I receive from nurses all week. The lactation consultant tells us that a scoop of ice cream floated in a pint of Guinness is a perfect post-breastfeeding snack, but the nurses in the general baby ed class tomorrow will tell us it's an old wives' tale that dark beers increase milk production and in fact we ought to avoid dehydrating beverages entirely. One nurse insists that the baby must be calm before latching, while another says it doesn't matter, then shoves my squalling infant onto my comically engorged breast, where she feeds hungrily for the next half hour. Cabbage leaves will bring that swelling down, says one nurse. Cabbage leaves dry up your milk supply, says the next. Some babies are sensitive to lanolin: Proceed with caution. Constantly slather your nipples in lanolin: Here are ten free samples. Sometimes, the advice divides along generations, but sometimes it follows no recognizable pattern. My partner and I start calling it *baby science*, this science that isn't science at all.

Or maybe, my thinking evolves, it's science fiction. Science fiction is what happens to you as you transform over nine months into an immunosuppressed host rearing to expel a writhing creature. Science and fiction combine to tell you how to care for it.

I haven't been paying attention. People are making moves to stand and the class is ending and where have I been? I'm tired in that bleary-eyed, lecture-hall way. My fiery brain begins to question itself. Maybe I'm not so immune to analysis; maybe the Percocet is wearing off already, taking my unearned confidence with it. In any case, I'm not so sure that I'll remember everything I'm supposed to do to keep my new animal alive.

So I wait until everyone shuffles out of the room and then I ask the lactation consultant if I can take a picture of the model baby, the cloth breast, correctly positioned. I figure that if I know this much, I'll probably be OK. The lactation consultant holds the models up to her chest again to demonstrate, fake breast over her real one, but concern flickers across her forehead as I take out my phone. "Just don't get my face in it, OK?"

I tell her I won't. She starts to say something, then stops, then starts again: "You're not going to use this in some weird porno, are you?"

I study her, looking for a sparkle in her eye, some sign that she is fucking with me. But there's nothing. She is *not* joking. She is seriously considering the possibility. And I am left wondering how anyone could possibly have the presence of mind—while swollen and bleeding and leaking at minimum two bodily fluids as they walk a thin tightrope over an ocean of breathtaking agony—to exhibit that kind of forethought?

I don't remember how I answer, but I remember being very tempted to say *Yes, yes I am. Would you mind signing this release form? Thanks so much for your participation in this project.*

I've sifted through my memory many times, panning for the precise postpartum moment when everything I understood about how to exist in the world shifted, when a fault line cracked open just wide enough for my childless self to slip through it without a sound. I'm not certain that this moment with the lactation consultant is it, but it seems like a contender.

I'd been afraid for years that all the sharp, bright edges of my life would be shorn off by motherhood. I'd imagined myself smothered in milky sweetness, drowned out by a white-noise hum of domesticity. Everything would become boring. I would become boring. But what I realize as I study the lactation consultant's humorless face is that everything is actually way weirder now that I've birthed someone. Everything will be at least a little strange from here on out. I don't know what it says about me that I'm comforted by the thought.

Marisa P. Clark

"The Beautiful Ones": Hattiesburg, 1986

I'd biked to the party, so I could drink, get drunk, not drive,
not have to stagger down the road in the wee-hours dark—
and then, fifth beer fizzing in a Solo cup, I met the eyes of a woman

staring in contempt, someone I'd seen that week at AA,
where I'd gone to support a friend new to sobriety. I took
a sip, licked foam from my lips, and "The Beautiful Ones"

came on: a song by Prince I liked to brood over in honor of
my ex, who'd stayed home that night. The woman's scathing gaze
felt like attack, so I escaped. In the kitchen, an old friend

from high school stood swaying, slugging her drink, flirting
with two men who lurked too near. One bragged that he'd be
getting lucky—and when he took her cup, to top it off, I warned,

"Drink lots of water. Take aspirin before you go to bed." I left
without finishing my beer. The world and my wheels wobbled,
so I rolled my bike beside me to prop me up. At home, my ex

had gone to bed. Her boyfriend's car was parked in the yard.
Next day, I told my sober friend about the woman who'd glared
with such begrudging judgment. Didn't she understand

that everyone struggled, everyone was prone to lapse,
and weren't we supposed to lend a helping hand? I felt
my failure then, not that I drank—my problem was never liquor—

but that I didn't stay with my old friend. In concert choir,
she'd sung first soprano, her voice bell-clear. If she'd met
with harm the night before, then shame on me, too busy courting

an opportunity to mourn my hapless love. My ex hadn't left
the porch light on. I chained my bike and fumbled for my key,
and the high notes of crickets pierced the night.

Autumn Schraufnagel

Joanne's Summer

Joanne sweats out entire seasons
at the community pool. Lemonade
and Leinenkugel in a tumbler
while the heat builds dizzy
on her skin. She, the very thing
that forces the forsaken pool to life—
winter's mess drained, rinsed, bleached.
Tarp and layer of muck water
peeled back for her painted toes
advertising a shade too bright
to believe. Shc is Best-Sky Blue.
She is Small-Town Expensive.
She is trauma at the edges of a brain
gone sparkly. Memory a nagging dog—
she is two divorces, a restraining order,
several domestic incidents—
men who sense she is childlike and simple.
Pool dads whose eyes cling to her
like burger drippings on a grill.
Even the birds queue up,
whistle from a telephone line
until summer sends its most insincere
9 p.m. sunset and Joanne retreats inside.
Even still, the frogs come out,
croak longer after summer rain
as if sadness were a necessity
in good lovemaking—
as if Joanne were, somehow, still near.

Autumn Schraufnagel

Coral Summers

Too young to be hurt by any of it—
incandescent Midwest, middle of the night
kissed with a waxy tongue.

Can't cling to any of it. Can't even say for sure
if I kissed only him. Deep freezer vodka bottles
we swapped with water—frozen adolescence

and evidence by morning. Empty house
of a night-shift nurse. Single mother
to our open-sky summer. Every weekend,

a different way to dress up another mistake.
Tonight—a backdrop of meteors falling
from the sky. A rush to the end

of their fiery lives. Back then, there was
an impossible stillness to each day—
and I'm sure she understood it, burning, too,

but in a different way. Hot summer,
blink of a mother. Coral bedroom
and every boyfriend that belonged to California.

Bedside Malibus and Coke.
Jenny knew every man in town with a boat.
Tanning beds and a '90s bust. She advised me

never to sleep through life. Galaxies away
in her backyard, while we smoked in the driveway,
drove her truck before a license,

ripped her window screens and scorched her carpets—
back then, the star-studded sky was still a backdrop.
Not the night blanket Jenny saw—big

and blameless. Space-black enough to shrink her,
and us, and every kind of fault.

Daniel Brennan

Pleasure as a Self-Fulfilling Prophecy

There's more to life than getting high.
I'm beginning to wonder if that's what you meant
when you said *Stay a little longer*. We've learned to lie

to each other, to our lovers; you and I
crowded in a dark, sour stall, our steady ascent,
as if there's nothing more to life than getting high.

The days are getting shorter, our evenings bone dry
and peeling with a headache. I'm reeling from minutes misspent
in this friction, these limbs. I don't want to lie,

but my pleasures are spelling out the ways that we die.
I tilt my head back; I give you my black-eyed consent.
Can there be more to life than getting high

off party favors in this club's liminal dark? We cry
out from the shadows, in rooms full of men bent
with prayerless peace. No escape now. Yes, we lie

every night. We lie in a body bag of promises. We sigh
and sag in our wanting. You're too good to me, sent
by bloodshot angels to distract me from the lie:
There's more to life than getting high.

Gabrielle Griffis

Beneath the Locust

The pullout couch was moldering. Green hyphae-stained foam cushions. Moss grew beneath upholstered fabric. A father and son carried the futon out to the woods after the boy tripped on the furniture's corner and smashed his teeth during one of their fights. Blood speckled the wall as he stumbled to the bathroom clutching his mouth. After the disposal, he and his friends used the sofa as a clubhouse fixture, clearing branches around the frame. They smoked weed and spray-painted boulders. Humidity swelled the cushions. Spring dew gave way to summer. Autumn leaves covered the bloated couch, and then a blanket of snow. When the weather warmed, ice dripped from the futon's edges, tainting the soil with flame retardant. In March, when the boy went to his clubhouse, the couch had lost all utility. The waterlogged seats smelled. The forest had taken over, fungus slowly consuming the fabric. His friends would visit a few more times, until their lives branched. His sister had been watching TV during the fight when her brother ran upstairs with a bloody mouth. Thunder rumbled. Summer rain poured into the pond, the marsh, flooding the swamp. A slurry of silt and mud flowed over moss. Locust branches took down power lines. When the lights came back on, the television did not. The house was quiet. The girl was unsure of what to do without smiles and songs. She swung on the swingset, pumping towards the clouds. In the forest, she pretended the TV still worked. She was the host of a documentary about squirrels. Nearby, their old refrigerator lay with the door-side up. The girl jumped into the appliance and pretended it was a boat. When her mother called her home, rain filled the compartment. Leaves and detritus fell into the cavity. Bugs skimmed the surface. Seasons elapsed, leaving layers of decay, algal blooms. Birds perched along the edge, plucking insects from the muddy pool. Her mother thought her father had brought the appliance to the dump, but he bought cigarettes and beer instead. He sat by the river, fishing and drinking with his son, a reprieve from their arguments. His son's grades slipped, he punched walls and smashed windows. The father threw tires and his daughter's mattress into the woods. The tires deteriorated slowly, the rims filled with pine needles, sticks, and plant debris. Leachate toxified the soil; oxidation dried the treads, which stiffened and cracked with the weather. The rusted springs of the mattress groaned. Dust rose and settled. Mice gnawed their way into the box spring, gathering fluff to line their nest. A great horned owl descended, sinking his talons into the mouse's fur. Stomach acid digested the rodent's body into a perfect skeleton, deposited somewhere in the duff. The mattress bloated and sagged, season after season. The girl grew up. She slept in other houses, other beds. The mattress continued to disintegrate. Her dreams dissolved with the rotting fibers. When her brother overdosed, she walked into the woods and stood over the remnants of the things her father dumped. She had forgotten about the fridge she used as a boat and her brother's couch. She wondered where their aspirations had been discarded if they landed in the dirt like broken objects. A great horned owl listened to her heartbeat. Moths hid under oak leaves. The fragrance of viburnum and mountain laurel floated through the air. Honeysuckle curled around rotted furniture; locust crowns snapped as salamanders regrew dismembered tails.

Mikki Aronoff

Blue Pieces of Sky

Stevie crawls out of bed tushy first, all Rubens pudge and pink, a mini-Michelin Man body. Stevie prefers to stay unfettered by clothes both in and outside his family's vine-covered Tudor cottage in the 1950s at the end of Rosebud Lane. On either side of the house, the Segals and Wards merely tsk tsk and draw drapes as the boy's father is a doctor and may be needed. He's a necessary neighbor, they whisper among themselves, unlike the wife. They watch Stevie's mother through the basement window. She has on only a skimpy painter's apron as she splashes abstractions on canvas, the floor, and herself. This morning, Stevie butt-bumps down the stairs for his oatmeal, toast and banana, the skin of which he peels into a floppy spider to give his babysitter. Mother grabs some shorts and a T-shirt for Stevie and a piano shawl to cover herself and bundles her son into the Plymouth. That afternoon, clothes back off, Stevie doesn't mention that Mrs. Foote picked up his spider with a rag and threw it into the trash. Stevie doesn't yet know the different words for sneering and looks that are askance. When he does, he will cry many rivers, but today he sits on the limestone steps that lead to the street and sings the song he just learned to the trilobites and crinoid stems trapped in stone's grip. His big sister gives him a look he can't yet interpret, so he sings again to the fossils. When he gets up, time is imprinted on his bottom.

Your brother shuffles into the kitchen at noon, one hand scratching his balding head, the other his crotch. Stevie's still in his pajamas. Chemo's maligned his tastebuds, and peanut butter's all he wants these days. You slap a slice of soft white bread onto the scuffed

Grand Canyon plate you found at the thrift shop, slather creamy peanut butter on top, try not to tear the bread. You leave the crust on, no jelly. Peaks and valleys form. Every day a new orogeny. Stevie, a paleontologist, taught you that word. You sit down with him at this week's jigsaw puzzle—yet another weathered barn—scattered across the kitchen table. In slow-motion, Stevie busies himself trying to match two blue pieces of sky. You watch him working the corners and the glands in your throat swell. He's so thin. You push the sandwich closer to him. He takes his index finger, zigzags a slow line across it. You startle as water begins to seep into the rivulet he's created. You lean over, dip a fingertip in. It tastes brackish. Stevie's staring deep into sticky peaks and salty currents, stays there.

Five months later, you wonder: When Stevie birthed that lagoon, did he jump in naked as the catfish and mollies and mudskippers who dwelled there? Did the tickle of fish and the swish of water return to him old memories of singing "The Itsy-Bitsy Spider?" Did he float on his back downstream, dream of freeing moss animals from rock?

Mikki Aronoff

How They Could Kick Us

Some crossed the river to settle in my hometown; others, continents. They made sausages, taught us the singsong of learning by rote. The streets smelled of fried catfish and pork, caraway and beer. The yeasty spoor of butternut bread baking for the city wafted over dressed geese and rockers on falling-down porches. There was a Chinese restaurant past our school by the pinball place on the main road that snaked through town. We worked flippers and tracked silver balls in their orbits until our parents dragged us back for steamy cashew chicken with rice in mounds scooped like ice cream. Lunchtimes at school, we wound around an old stone fountain next to the cafeteria to wet our hands before eating. Our fourth-grade music teacher taught us to play "I'm Dreaming of a White Christmas" on tonettes. Once, she asked me to fetch something, and I found a half-drunk glass of Hudepohl in her desk drawer, foam still on top. I didn't tell on her because we didn't tell on anyone. That's how things could keep happening. The vice principal snapping his cane over the bent backs of rowdy boys in gym, with its polished wood floors and shivers of young bodies. How we learned to detect the sweat of tweed, how bullies got even with their world. How one day they could kick us because they never saw us cry, and the next day we'd be back to drawing cartoons in basement bedrooms or catching crawdads in the creek behind our houses. That was when we learned to flaunt or hide our young breasts, to consecrate all the town's fountains with the steam of our bodies. That was when we raced bicycles across the tracks, over to the cemetery, breathless, knowing the wrong boys would catch us there, but the dead couldn't.

Teresa Buzo Salas

Vegetative Love

My Love:

Just about every week, I write a letter to tell you every little thing that happens, so that when you wake up you won't feel as though you've missed out on anything. Like someone once said, life is an open book full of blank pages for us to write in, but don't you worry, because I'm filling yours with my own words.

If you could only see how big the girls have gotten! Our oldest is nearly as tall as me, and the youngest reaches up to my waist. Right now, she is making a drawing for you, to hang in your hospital room next to the others. She's so excited that she rubs her wax crayon sticks over the sheet with all her little strength, staining the kitchen table with blue scratches. As I look at her, I see me, trying to paint a soul that has become a blank, a soul that is now empty and that rings hollow on nights when I cannot be by your side, though it fills again with rainbows when I visit you in the morning.

In the drawing, the four of us are strolling in the park, under a sun that's round and very yellow. It's strange. She usually draws you lying on the hospital bed, because she does not remember you any other way. Yet, this time, she is drawing you standing up. She says she saw it in a dream. How I wish it would come true. How I wish that we could one day go to the park, the four of us together, under a yellow sun, or an orange or red one, but all of us together, so we can chat and laugh, and—why not?—even argue. How you always believed that you were so absolutely right. And that absolute and sometimes-wicked rightness led you to lie flat in a hospital bed. But I don't want to talk about that now. Better if I talk about us, about the things that we will do then, when this long and tedious waiting marked with desolate green hallways, sanitizer, and bland meals is over.

I'm sorry to tell you that yesterday, again, I got upset with the nurse. She says that I shouldn't spend every night in the hospital, that my back must be thrown from sleeping in that chair. She says that I have enough with working and picking up the girls from my mother's to take them to school. She even dared to tell me that I'm neglecting home and that the circles under my eyes hang like two brown doves, fat and stiff. What would she know about doves! I feel them resting on my breasts when I sleep holding your hand. My body beats like wings when it senses a pulse in your wrist, that delicious melody, your blood attuned to the same rhythmic cadences, encouraging, alive … what would she know!

Tomorrow is Sunday, so while the girls go out with friends, I will stay with you. I remember how I used to tell you that Sunday was the only day of the week that feels like casting an anchor on a heap of nothings. You did not understand me, so I explained that Sundays are like barren plains after stepping out of a jungle of unending comings and goings, and doings. And in the middle of that barrenness, nostalgia settles in. Those mornings I lounged in bed curled up like a baby, hugging the pillows. Your arms around me, you pulled me tight against your chest, as if to sift me inside you so as to never let me go. Moments later, you began to kiss me, your breath sour and dry but, for me, tasting like bread just out of the oven, like hot coffee and glory cakes. Everything is different now. Sundays no longer seem like empty plains ridged with affection. My world centers around the amount of time I can spend being by your side. Running through the calendar for a holiday that will free me from the yoke of work, so I may leave and run straight to the hospital with my heart in my mouth because I've sensed a heartbeat. It's true that in the span of these eight years, hope has been my loyal companion, that green path of poets in love who go on strolling without turning back—it's been with me, always.

Without a doubt, the most sublime moment of the day is when I bathe you. I almost had to sue the clinic because they would not let me do it alone. Everything was a problem because I needed the help of a professional, because you were too heavy for me to turn you over without help, and another thousand nonsenses that I've had to listen to. Of course. What do doctors know about intimacy! They are used to slashing open and exposing the viscera of their patients to their surgical staff. Who better than me to attend to your care? I know every inch of your skin, as if your body were a map with clues and keys to a treasure. A magnificent fount of fortune you are, my love, you and only you. I can mentally place every freckle, every tiny wrinkle and bristly hair on your chest, now even better than before, and I enjoy contemplating your whole body while I undress you, removing your garments with skill and calm. I wish to be the breeze that delicately snatches strands of straw from the dry wheat fields. In those moments, while I pluck each one of your petals, you cease being my husband and become my offspring. A child I care for and speak to in that baby talk that mothers use to nurture the soul with light and guidance.

This is how I spend every evening of this summer, sprinkling powdered sugar over an unjust bitterness. A thick bile that rises to my throat and leaves an acrid taste, repulsive yet sufferable. But, I don't want that taste of bile to dissolve entirely, because nothing frightens me more than to stop feeling disgust for this iniquity that has been inflicted upon you. I refuse to get used to it. I refuse to drag my existence through that dreary course, to turn into a matron on autopilot, hardened by routine. I want my soul to hurt like it did the first day, so I can keep confronting this adversity.

Nights are always worse than mornings, especially on those mornings when I cannot be with you. On those deafening nights when the silence takes over the house and the shadows wander through the hallways, I open your closet and I slip my face between your shirts. I stop breathing for a few seconds. Then, nearly fainting, I inhale with all my strength to sense your aroma and to imagine that you are holding me. I do it right before I go to sleep, when I've already put on my pajamas and I've turned off the night lamp. That way, when I shut the closet, I slip under the covers while wrapped in your scent. Sometimes, insomnia wakes me up in the middle of the night and I find myself on your side of the bed, but I quickly turn away because that's your side and it continues to be so.

I know that one of these days, they will call me. They will give me good or bad news. I know that it could happen in a day or in fifty years. And I also know that no matter what happens, I have to stay strong for the girls. In the meantime, my love, I take care of you, and I will continue to fill with my words the pages of this blank book that defines your life and mine.

Translated from the Spanish by Laura Valeri

Alex Juffer

Stars So Close You Could Hit One With a Prayer

The children stopped speaking. They were put on bed rest.

The local fracking conglomerate was blamed at first, along with the middle-school reading curriculum, which featured a dystopian Young Adult book in which a group of teenage rebels learned sign language, forsaking the traditional language, to evade detection by the oppressive government.

The books were quietly shuffled a town over. The fracking company donated ten thousand dollars to the children's hospital and bought lunch for all the nurses.

The children stopped eating. The medical specialists resorted to feeding tubes. Distressed mothers protested. The medical staff added food coloring to the nutrients coursing through the feeding tubes to suggest personalized flavors. They took fictitious orders. The mothers relented.

The small urgent-care center, overwhelmed, set up pop-up cots—leftover from the hurricane scare—on the high school basketball court. There were over fifty children, lined up in rows of ten. The children stared; they were said to be greedy with eye contact. Some parents blindfolded their own children during visiting hours.

The mayor called upon the advice of a preeminent child psychologist, a religious leader, and an artist who specialized in mass-scale spectacles and whose medium, he claimed, was the human body.

The child psychologist slept in the gym on a cot, tirelessly studying the children. His conclusive findings suggested they start over from childbirth and bring in new mothers to breastfeed the stupefied patients, progressing later to diapers and simple gestures.

The artist scoffed. He said that it was clear that God wanted these children dead and that to intervene was folly. The artist offered to entomb the children where they lay, in plaster, turning the gymnasium into a museum, a cautionary tale of "the nadir of social media and the severance between body and mind." In private, the artist confided that he already had the name for the exhibit: *The Living Graveyard*.

The religious leader, to the surprise of everyone, agreed with the artist.

None of the options seemed palatable.

The children stopped moving, lying stock-still in their cots, muscles petrified, like a brigade of soldiers training in their sleep. City council sought out the psychologist, ready to try anything, but he had fled in the middle of the night.

People came from all over to pray and leave teddy bears outside the gym. Always teddy bears. Despite initial resistance, the exhausted nurses let the worshippers in to dab clean sponges on the foreheads of the children, to massage feeling back into their feet.

Even with constant care, the children slipped into comas. The police escorted the artist out, while the nurses found themselves responsible for dragging the fervent devotees out. The doors were padlocked, the school condemned.

The worshippers came back in the night, climbing onto the roof, circling around the vents directly over the gymnasium. It was a cool, clear, dark night, ideal for prayer.

They waited for the sweet, putrid smell of dead flesh, but they were prepared for it to never come.

B. Luke Wilson

The Wolves of Chernobyl

April 2003, Ukraine

"Too much radiation ahead," Igor shouted over the roar of the bus engine. "It is bad for the liver to mix such air with food. Better to eat now, before we reach the exclusion zone!" His deliberate English cut through the wool of a heavy Slavic accent. He repeated these instructions in Ukrainian, the syllables sharper.

Outside my window, the village of Lyutizh glided past with only the golden cross of the famous Khram Rizdva Presvyatoyi Bohorodytsi church visible through the fog. As others on the bus ate, my gaze returned to the strange artifact that Igor had strapped to the floor behind his gearshift. A toddler car seat sat beneath his elbow, with a green Soviet-era Geiger counter buckled inside. For miles, I'd been mesmerized by this strange pairing. I couldn't remember the last time I'd felt that protected. Igor's fingers began to caress the Geiger counter's chipped surface. I looked away. I hated watching tenderness.

Soon, the air was filled with the savory aromas of clove and cumin. The tour group ate, their voices bubbling together into a thick stew of Slavic languages. My Russian and Ukrainian were fluent, leaving the other dialects a mystery. No other journalists were on the bus, and I stood out with my camera bag and American accent. Tonight was the seventeenth anniversary of the meltdown; maybe they were returning home.

Across the median, a military convoy approached us as it headed south toward Kyiv. A hulking KrAZ heavy utility truck led the procession, its sharp headlights lancing through the fog. Since childhood, bright headlights had always had a horrible effect on me—and my pulse started to churn as a familiar panic teethed beneath my throat. A wolf cub broke out of the woods into the road, and the truck devastated the vanishing softness of its body.

I took a long drink from a bottle of Gatorade I had mixed with vodka, trying not to look at the smear the cub left over the asphalt. This wasn't the time for another breakdown. In two days, I would be home. I stared at Igor's Geiger counter, safe inside its little nest, and forced myself to count out slow breaths. The bottle emptied. Gradually, the panic in my throat dissolved back into bile.

I awoke at the Pripyat checkpoint to Igor's fingers jabbing into my ribs. He wore the tacklebox-sized Geiger counter strapped across a large belly.

"Are you the journalist then, Adam?" Igor demanded. "A man from your office called yesterday. Is this what I should have expected, a drunk asleep on my bus?" Middle-aged and balding, Igor had the buzzing manic energy of a televangelist.

"Sorry, just jet lag, that's all," I said. Nobody else at my travel magazine spoke Ukrainian. If they did, I would still be in Atlanta. I spoke four languages; they needed me too much to fire me. Gathering my duffle and camera bag, I hurried off the bus.

The checkpoint was little more than a roadblock surrounded by a few drab single-story buildings. Beyond a flimsy gate loomed the ghost town of Pripyat, where rows of khrushchyovka apartment buildings crumbled into the ground. A young guard shouldered his AK-47 and checked me for radiation. In brutally candid Ukrainian, he told me one millisievert was an acceptable daily dose of radiation inside the city. Above that was, as he said, *not compatible with living.*

Igor disappeared into a cinderblock building while the tour group chatted outside. A graying couple told me they had traveled all the way from Latvia to celebrate their fortieth anniversary among the rubble. God bless them, I suppose. Maybe their fondness for each other felt stronger while standing beneath mountains of broken things.

"You are British?" the Latvian man asked in broken English.

"No, American," I said.

"Ah, Yankee. You here for pictures?" He gestured at my camera bag. I explained that my travel magazine had sent me to interview and photograph the local residents, the Samosely. They had lived in Pripyat since long before the 1986 meltdown and afterward ignored the government mandate and remained in the radioactive city. Igor's tour of Pripyat was a formality; the interviews didn't begin until tonight. On paper, my article would celebrate the Samosely and their stories of rugged survival. In truth, my editor had already told me only the pictures mattered, not what they had to say. I was there for their faces.

I drifted away from the group to where a few Ukrainian men were smoking behind a wall of sandbags. I bummed a smoke off a tall man in a Nirvana concert hoodie who introduced himself as Artyom. He leaned against the sandbags, wolflike brown hair corralled into a loose ponytail. A crescent of fresh razor burn ran across his neck like a noose. Between deep drags on an unfiltered Prima, he explained that he worked at the Hotel Desyatka and sometimes helped Igor with the tours. Artyom quickly noticed that my hands were shaking. I needed a stiff drink every few hours. He offered to top off my flask, which was down to the dregs.

"Never drink the last sip," Artyom said, pouring from his bottle. "All the metal in the flask, the nickel, the tin, gets soaked up in the last sip. Like a bit of bread at the bottom of your soup. *That's* what gives the hangover." He tapped his temple. "And don't mind Igor," Artyom continued. "He lost a son who was still a boy; now he drinks more than both of us together."

My flask was half filled when Igor burst out of the building and stomped in our direction. "Artyom, pospishaty," Igor shouted. "No one pays you to smoke!" Cursing, I hid my flask behind the wall. Artyom and I stubbed out our smokes and joined the rest of the group.

Igor started the tour with a warning: Parts of the city were still dangerously radioactive. His rough fingers stroked the Geiger counter as he spoke. Our group floated off on his caution, moving through the central square. The skyline towered over us like a broken jaw full of rotten teeth.

We stopped at the entrance hall to the Palace of Culture Energetik. A vibrant mural bloomed across the bare concrete showing a circle of people embracing with their heads bowed, a woman in blue carrying a basket of oranges, and a man holding a white scroll. His face was peeling away. Igor noticed a knot of fur stuck to a piece of exposed rebar, and he plucked the hair with surprising grace. In a voice booming inside the hall, Igor spoke of the wolves in the hills, how they were as tall as a man's shoulder and could bite through a chain-link fence. This, Igor claimed, was their fur. Artyom smirked at these words, chest thrown out like a shield.

Igor taunted him with the clump of hair. "You'd love to hold a lucky piece like this, wouldn't you, Artyom? The great wolves are everywhere at night, except where you look." Igor laughed, tucking the fur into his pocket.

"Forget him," Artyom mumbled to me.

The tour ended a few hours later at the Pripyat cemetery, where a gray granite obelisk had been built in memory of those who died controlling the meltdown. I thought it was as noble a way to die as any other. Some people posed for photos in front of the monument, but nobody knew what to do with their hands. One good-natured woman smiled and made a peace sign. Then she somehow thought better of it, crossing her arms instead. Artyom nodded toward her. "People," he mumbled. "People worry too much about things that change nothing."

After the tour, Igor steered his bus southeast toward the Hotel Desyatka. The fading light clung to the rust grotesquely. I sat beside Artyom and skimmed through an address book before my interviews with the Samosely. As I muttered through my notes, Artyom recognized one of the names. His mother was Samosely, and he knew many others. I explained my assignment to him. That evening, I was scheduled to visit a dozen Samosely apartments and collect photographs of their faces. The more austere the inhabitants and dilapidated the buildings, the better.

"I know the city good as anyone," Artyom said. "I would drive you for, what, fifty euros?"

I would rather ride with him than whatever chauffeur my magazine had arranged. We shook on it as the bus slowed at another checkpoint outside the village of Leliv.

At the Hotel Desyatka, an oil painting of the Mother of God of Yaroslavl hung over my bed. It showed the Mother with child held to her cheek; one of his hands clutched her collar and the other her chin—although she cradled him with such strength, there was no reason for him to be holding on. I thought about my mom. It would be around midnight in Atlanta; she was probably sleeping.

I refilled my flask from a liter of Moskovskaya in my duffel. I had wrapped each liter in a sweater to mute that strange, oily music that liquor bottles tended to make whenever they clinked together. Once settled, I didn't turn on the TV. I wanted to disappear into the exactness of nothing. I drank and stared out the window, where darkness swelled like an abscess.

That evening, Artyom drove me along the Pripyat River from one small Samosely village to another. He sang old Ukrainian folk songs in a voice high and beautiful.

The Samosely interviews blurred together. They had been either too old or too stubborn to resettle after the meltdown. Besides, many of them had lived through both the Holodomor Famine and the Nazi occupation. They were accustomed to calamity. For the last interview, we drove to the outskirts of a village where an old Samosely man lived alone in a plywood hovel. His luminous green eyes were set like craters beneath the wild topography of a rutted brow, and their light screamed a stark contrast to the black fur of his Cossack hat. He was precisely what my magazine wanted. I tried to explain to the old man that I needed his photograph, but he just stared at me, saying something in a dialect I didn't understand.

"He is offended you do not look him in the eyes," Artyom translated softly into English. "He says it is disrespect to enter a man's home without meeting his eyes." I stared up into the old man's gaze. His eyes were beautiful but almost to the point of becoming cruel, and I didn't understand how something so gentle had survived here.

On our way back to the hotel, Artyom invited me to his mother's apartment for dinner. He'd moved in a few years ago, after Yana got too old to look after herself. At their apartment, Yana insisted on making me elderberry tea. She was dressed in all blue except for the sun-drenched yellows and golds of her babushka. As she lit the brass samovar, I noticed her fingernails were missing. Where the nails should have been was only stretched skin, giving her hands the appearance of weathered gloves. I wondered if she'd been interrogated during the Great Terror, although she smiled as though she'd never felt pain.

We ate borscht with pampushki rolls for dipping and candied sweet oranges. I couldn't remember the last time I'd felt like part of a family. Yana had taught English at a local grammar school, and she told stories of Artyom's childhood in her clear and resonant English. His favorite toy had been a stuffed elephant that he'd named Slon, Ukrainian for elephant.

"Of all the names for a toy!" Yana's voice shimmered. "Why name a thing exactly the thing it is? What should I have named you, then?"

Artyom nodded. "It was a fine name and a fine toy. And you could have named me anything. These things don't matter."

Yana stayed up with us after dinner, playing bura and other card games. I tried not to look at her fingers. Artyom let her win, and by the second round, I'd caught on and did the same. I thought about my mom; maybe this would be the year I visited her. I would have to dry out first. We'd reached the unspoken agreement that I wouldn't see her again until I got sober. It had been at least three years. Maybe four. My mind drifted to the totality of circumstances standing between me and her front porch. Even if I made it there, what then? A silence existed between us, one made constant by a shared history neither of us could speak, unmovable whether we were separated by the distance of my arm or by entire continents.

Around ten o'clock, Yana retired to her room while Artyom and I kept playing cards and drinking. His tales grew bolder with the night. Soon, he was telling magnificent stories of his father's time in the Ukrainian Insurgent Army. His dad had been a local folk hero during the war, fighting for Ukrainian sovereignty against both the Russians and Germans. Artyom's voice swelled with pride. His father had been captured near the Polish border in 1943 and survived years of torture in the gulags without ever saying a word. He returned after the war and lived well into his sixties. I thought about Yana's fingernails—she must have also held her silence.

"Enough games." Artyom slammed his cards on the table. "You ever been hunting, Adam?"

"Sure," I replied. "I hunted as a kid. Deer hunting with my uncles."

"Did your dad hunt?" Artyom asked.

I weighed how much to tell him. "My dad wasn't around long. He was an asshole."

"Most of my friends are assholes," Artyom said. "I am sure there was some good in him."

"Well, he told great dirty jokes," I admitted. "I bit my fingernails as a kid. He told me once, 'I bet you like biting your nails because it scratches on the way out.'"

Artyom laughed. "See, that is something. What else? Tell another of his jokes."

"That's the only one that stuck with me," I said. "He went to jail when I was six." I remembered bright headlights, hard knuckles the size of clam shells—then a long drive to a new apartment with thin walls that never held any heat.

"Six?" he said earnestly. "A shame so young."

"I still had my mom," I said. "She always kept us fed, even after we were evicted."

"She must be a strong woman." Artyom nodded. These words sat a moment in the air, undigested.

"To mothers!" Artyom toasted. We drank in silence for a long time. I thought about my mom. About Yana. About silence as an act of bravery. Maybe I was brave for not telling him why my dad had gone to jail. For carrying that myself.

"Well, what did you shoot?" Artyom asked at last. "With the uncles? A Remington? Marlin? You ever shot a real gun?"

"I've shot a 12-gauge and a deer rifle. And, well, let's see …."

He smiled. "You stay right here, friend. I will show you a *real* gun."

Artyom returned soon, a wide, shit-eating grin on his face. He had a submachine gun in each hand, a drum-fed PPSh-41 *papasha* in his right, a weapon similar to the AK-74 in his left.

"These are my girls," Artyom said. "Meet Vera and Nina." He raised each weapon with its introduction. "So, tell me, do you want to go hunting?"

"What's there to hunt at midnight in the exclusion zone?" I laughed.

"The wolves, Adam." Artyom was at once dead serious. "Great, strong, powerful beasts. The radiation kills the weak ones but makes the strong ones stronger. Their eyes glow green at night, and Adam, never in the world has there been a stronger good-luck charm. Whatever it is you want in life: women, power, fame. Just a strand of their hair is enough. Enough for all of it. What say you?"

"With machine guns?" I asked, dumbfounded. "Isn't there a curfew? And radiation?" Even as I argued, I wanted a reason to say yes.

"Forget the curfew," Artyom insisted. "We drive without headlights. And the radiation? I know the city, the spots to avoid. The Red Forest has many wolves but, yes, more radiation. Spiders there spin odd little webs, they are so scrambled with it. But, along the Uzh River, less wolves, less radiation." Artyom tore a piece of Yana's stationery off a pad and sketched a crude map over the embossed wrens and roses.

"The nearest fork of the Uzh is southeast and not far to travel. Radiation is not so bad there. Better with a Geiger counter, but we will be fine."

With that, I was ready. I grabbed the map and stuffed it into my pocket. "Take me to the hotel, Artyom. I will get you a Geiger counter."

A childish grin spread across Artyom's face. He nodded.

I drank from a half-empty bottle as Artyom drove us to the Hotel Desyatka. He knew the night worker and bribed him for Igor's room key. Igor snored naked in his bed, with one arm unfurled at his side. There were no bottles in his room; Artyom had been mistaken. Igor was bone sober. The Geiger counter sat on a nightstand beside the bed, inches from his outstretched fingers. Next to it rested a photo of Igor as a young man—showing him cradling his baby son in front of a waterfall while a pretty brunette woman beamed next to them. The car seat on Igor's bus would have fit the boy perfectly. I tried not to think about it.

Artyom and I drove off toward the Uzh River with two submachine guns, Igor's green box, a couple of flashlights, and a liter of excellent Nemiroff. Without the burden of headlights, his blue Volvo slipped through the vacant streets. Windows down, the night air was a silence stitched from thousands of tiny noises. It sounded like the shape of the universe, a maelstrom of wings, great and small, all beating together.

We parked beside the road and walked southwest through a spruce forest along the Uzh River. The Nemiroff was much finer vodka than Artyom was used to, and he was slamming it back. I had Igor's box turned on and strapped across my chest. Whenever the beeps got closer together, we would stumble the other way. In this manner, we zigzagged along with our flashlights, hunting the great wolves.

We roamed for three hours like this, eventually reaching the top of a bluff overlooking the river. The lowest fringe of sky was already turning from black to a bruised mauve. I wanted to turn back, but Artyom insisted. We wandered another half hour along the river. Finally, I saw them. Three gray wolves were a short distance ahead of us—lurking right against the hem of the tree line. We crouched, sinking down as if one being. Artyom was wrong; the wolves had yellow eyes, not green.

"Aim for the smallest one," Artyom breathed. "If they run, he will be slowest. Ready? One, two—"

My finger towed down the cold trigger, rupturing the peaceful night air. A host of birds erupted from the trees as one of the wolves collapsed into the grass.

Artyom and I rushed over. The fallen wolf looked half starved, emaciated even, but Artyom was crying. "He's beautiful, Adam. Can you see him? Can you see what a beast he is?"

Artyom cut a clump of fur off the animal with the menacing edge of his knife. He handed the tuft to me as if it were a trophy. I slipped the hair into my breast pocket and felt nothing—no warmth or satisfaction. The clouds shifted, illuminating the wolf for the first time. It looked pitiful, barely an adult, with mangy fur clotted into knots. Scars crisscrossed its neck from fights lost to stronger wolves. But, Artyom acted like he was seeing an entirely different creature. His muscles shivered with exertion as he knelt before the carcass. A few tears streaked down his face before he turned to hide them from me. I pretended to see the same great beast that he did.

It took half an hour to drag the wolf back to Artyom's car. Once there, we started celebrating, drinking hard and fast. Far off down the road, I saw headlights coming toward us from the hotel. As they got closer, I recognized Igor's bus. Wasted and impetuous on the hunt, I aimed my AK-74 up into the night sky and squeezed back on the trigger. Artyom slapped my barrel down, cursing from deep inside his lungs. "Blyat!" he slobbered. "Don't shoot. That's the army!" He struggled to stand, swaying over the dark river of pavement.

"No, it's Igor. See. See, his bus—." As I raised the gun to point, my finger somehow slipped over the trigger. One final blast rang out, and Artyom crumpled to the ground.

"Artyom!" I shouted, dropping down beside him. He only looked surprised. Touching his leg just above the knee, he marveled at the fresh blood.

"It doesn't hurt," he mumbled. "It just feels warm. Maybe warm with needles below."

Then I saw Artyom's eyes. His pupils were sinking down into his skull. If the bullet had hit an artery, we didn't have much time.

"Did you see me?" Artyom winced a smile. "Did you see me shoot the wolf? It was my shot that took him. Yours went high. It was *my* shot. Did you, did you see it, Adam? Did you ...." His voice faded down to a wet gurgling.

"I saw it," I said. "I saw it!" It scared me how he sounded almost like a child now. I tried to put pressure on the wound, but an impossible amount of blood had already escaped his body.

Suddenly, Igor was beside me on the road, with Artyom's stationery map clutched in his fist. It must have fallen out of my pocket in his room. He grabbed the strap of the Geiger counter and started to swear at me for stealing it. Then he saw Artyom and shouted, dropping down beside us.

Without asking what had happened, Igor twisted his belt into a tourniquet and wrapped it above the wound, then he removed the cleaning rod from my AK-74 and used it as a windlass to twist the belt down toward bone. Artyom struggled weakly against him, making horrible, broken sounds.

"The Army will be here soon," Igor said as he tied down the cleaning rod. "We are close enough to the city. They must have heard the shots. Tell me now, Adam. Tell me true. Did you shoot him, or was it himself?"

"It was me," I said. My tongue felt too thick for words. "I didn't mean to—a misfire—my finger slipped—"

"This is the wrong country to shoot a man," Igor said urgently. "It doesn't matter how. We must hide his gun. Throw it deep in the woods. With one gun, they may believe he shot himself, drunk as you both are."

"Why are ... why are you helping me?" I garbled.

"Because you are a child," Igor replied. He grabbed Artyom's papasha and hurried toward the tree line.

Kneeling in the road, I slipped the lucky wolf hair Artyom had given me into his breast pocket. Then I placed his cold hand over it. His fingers clutched around the fur, holding onto the wolves of Chernobyl—their myth, their luck, their silence ... I didn't know. After he stopped breathing, I sat there listening to the stars.

Igor saved me. When the Ukrainian soldiers arrived, he lied, telling them he found me carrying Artyom out of the woods. He told them Artyom accidentally shot himself hunting and I'd done my best to save him. Half of that was true. The soldiers loaded Artyom into a military ambulance, and they raced away toward the first light of dawn.

Igor drove me back to his small office. We waited for the news. I spent those hours rocking myself inside the thin jaw of a folding chair. Artyom was pronounced dead around 9 a.m. at a nearby field hospital. I wished to be blameless—a bystander who had witnessed something irrevocable and eternal. But, I knew my shot had killed him. By late afternoon, I was sober enough to stand, and a rawboned Ukrainian lieutenant told me to leave the country and never come back.

That evening, Igor drove me to the Kyiv airport. My hands trembled with such violence, I almost dropped my camera bag. But, I didn't dare to drink in front of him, not after the previous night. I begged him to stop at Yana's apartment, just long enough for me to give her some money and explain what had happened. But, his agreement with the guards had been to make no stops until we were outside the exclusion zone. I called my mom when he stopped for petrol in Khocheva. She didn't pick up. It would be 1 a.m. in Atlanta; she was probably sleeping. I left a message saying I was fine and heading home.

We reached Kyiv by dusk. Outside the airport, Igor offered me a cigarette, and we smoked while watching the planes. He took his old Geiger counter out of a knapsack and cradled it, almost lovingly. One side was collapsed in like a crushed milk carton; I must have dropped it sometime in the night. He said the device was a family heirloom from his father, who had used it all those years ago, during the meltdown.

Igor took a long drag off his cigarette. "I think you should keep it. The Geiger counter."

"Why?" I asked.

Igor considered. "Look at it. What use is it to me now? Maybe it will remind you of what happened. I would rather you carry it than the weight of this happening again. You did something terrible, Adam. It will live in you forever."

I stared at the ruined device as tears welled up in my eyes. I hated how it felt to cry in front of him. Hated how it proved beyond doubt the helplessness Igor had already seen in me. I wanted to refuse his charity in two graveled syllables, march straight-backed and proud into the airport, and fly home without another thought of him. But, I couldn't.

"What do I do now?" I pleaded.

Igor shook his head. "Go home. Then find a mirror and ask that again."

After Igor left, I sat on the curb beside his Geiger counter and gulped vodka until my body stopped shaking. I hadn't had a drink since the night before, and the electric tremors of withdrawal were surging up my arms. I needed to forget. But, a bottomless dread burned beneath my throat like a molten rock I couldn't swallow or spit out. A good man would still be alive if not for me. And his saint of a mother would have to survive without a son, without anyone to care for her. Artyom might have said worrying changes nothing, but he wasn't the one who had to keep living. I would have given anything to trade places with him.

My fingers explored the Geiger counter's cold metallic skin. Igor's kindness somehow hurt as much as Artyom's death. I didn't deserve it. I slammed the rest of the bottle against the curb. The glass shattered, and only the tawny label tried to hold the broken pieces together. And nobody could hate it for that. For holding on. It didn't know how to do anything else.

Katy Aisenberg

Rat

For my husband could cut my arm off, cut my feet off. Just leave the body.
The surgeon said I scar well. Save my marriage to the end.
See something to the end, a John Wayne sunset.
We slept like stacked apartments. People can't say
there wasn't love—we were true—blue bodies in one bed.
Animals in that house were uneasy. Previous tenants buried a twin.
The rat's grinning face and pale hairless tail scurried in
while my husband was away. I locked the nursery door.
A flying squirrel died in the wall. The cat ran away on Christmas Eve.
Dodged a bullet, they all said, but I had spent my thicket life
painting my eyes gentian blue like Liz Taylor like Anne of Cleaves,
my head gone and all for love. Dodged a bullet they all said.
But I want one metallic sweet to suck. Want to be undone.
I handed my husband a thread from my sweater and said pull,
pull & walk away.

Shyla Shehan

She Paid No Mind

Every autumn I walk melancholy
in the garden center at the hardware store
through mostly emptied pallets and dried-up mums
pleading for a change of scenery

In the garden center at the hardware store
a sense of loss washes in
Pleading for a change of scenery
reminds me of a girl I used to know

A sense of loss washes in
chill of wind through chain-link fences
reminds me of a girl I used to know
who kicked her heels out on the swing set at the school

Chill of wind through chain-link fences
shadows growing longer around the girl
who kicked her heels out on the swing set at the school
then skipped along cracked sidewalks to her home

Shadows growing longer around the girl
she knew it meant the sun was soon to set
then skipped along cracked sidewalks to her home
falling leaves skittered across her path

She knew it meant the sun was soon to set
Another year tumbles toward the end
falling leaves skittered across her path
She paid no mind to mums along the way

Nicole Markert

Autocorrect Changes "I'm Yelling" to "I'm Yellowing"

I think of smoker's teeth with coffee
        stains in the cracks. The honey-colored

moon in June. The bees & the crisp daffodils.
        How they plume pollen into the air.

Yellowing comes with age,
        & I think about the stem of my spine.

Bones will yellow while still in the body
        if we let them, like expired milk in the fridge,

the crumpled dog-eared newspaper
        with my brother's obituary

& the old Polaroid I gave my old love
        (if I can even call him that).

I forced the relationship to walk before it was able,
        like a fresh foal on soft hooves.

My mother tells me I should find a man
        before my eyes yellow like a cat's.

She wants a grandson before she withers.
        She never speaks of women.

She tells me my feelings are dandelion seeds,
        They will blow away.

Nathan D. Metz

In Some Lights

Untitled, *Mark Rothko, 1969*

Nights stack dull like thick slabs. You woke up late
    and late for nothing. Gray clouds rain gray

rain, catches in the smog and spices your city
    sour, street lamps and headlights proving the black

of space more apparent. Rothko wanted to paint
    about death, traced a thin line keeping black from gray.

You don't know which of the colors is death. It could
    be both. God sits and observes from his black-

and-white TV and is bored, the picture fuzzy,
    the sound off. He is just guessing. Gray

is a hesitation that begins when squeezed
    between absolutes. When your friend died, everyone wore black

and told stories and they were all love stories
    and they were all ghost stories. The day's gray

rhythm kept ticking on death's time. Rothko
    was stubborn and purposefully placed darker

colors on top to keep viewers from mistaking
    his moods of color for landscapes, for tangibility, the chunk of
        gray

nothing but flat grayness, black flat blackness.
It didn't work. Some patrons said he must have painted a blurred black-

and-white photo, or, given the year 1969,
a lunar landing, that he painted that cold gray

surface of nothing to critique such a finish line.
It is late winter. Thursday. Your friend died eleven black

days ago. You don't know where he is.
Rothko wanted to paint about death, huge gray

under huge black, but it never would have worked.
At the exhibit tomorrow, you will see the slabbed black

over slabbed gray, and you will stare with suspicion
for a while, a long while, and studying that thick grayness

you will swear, despite and through Rothko,
that somewhere off canvas, maybe in the darkest

corner of his studio, Rothko painted a moon,
not the idea of a moon or mood of a moon but a moon, huge white

and pushing light through low fog,
the painting around you gray, in some lights, silver.

Andrew Stancek

The Last Bird

After Father ran off with Helga the Trapeze Artist and Mother was bundled off to the Přelouč Home for the Insane, I moved in with Aunt Elvira, ready to embrace my destiny.

At fifteen I was a year too young for Emperor Franz's Army and eight years too old to undertake training as a contortionist with the Brno Circus. Life with Elvira, twenty years older than Mother, and twenty times more adventurous, would have to suffice until I soared.

Elvira woke me every morning with an operatic aria or a gruesome tale. Our family always starred: cousins and aunts, grandfathers and grandmothers, an intricate web going generations back—lives exploding with adventure, fortunes gained and lost, stabbings and hangings, weddings and betrayals, deaths.

Her mother, Elvira said, bereft at losing her husband, threw herself into a pond, changed her mind, swam to shore and married Mayor Slavek. Two brothers went off to war, never to be seen again. Five sisters died: diphtheria, childbirth, flu, drowning, fire. "And your mother—ach, you poor child—the less said, the better."

She adored her radio opera broadcasts, conducted madly with both arms, wept and cackled at gypsy curses, enslaved maidens, lost heirs, abortive rescues, prophecies, executions. She sang throughout the day, sometimes accompanying her gramophone, more frequently a capella. As if I were the cause of Carmen's tragic death, she glared and bellowed, "Mort, mort."

Early mornings I set out to catch carp in Marian Pond, dreaming of sharks. I gamboled through the county seat's twisty alleys, drinking in the catcalls of the women in upper windows. Hour after hour, from high up a poplar, I watched as soldiers marched outside the barracks, uniform buttons gleaming, bayonets pulsing with blood. The vultures in the trees lining the alley cawed, certain of carrion. I stared with longing into the window of Sratschka's Pawn Shop, where a hat and regimental colors accompanied an officer's sword, the hilt worn, the blade expectant. I considered breaking the window to grab the glory but suspected I'd be captured and shamed as a petty criminal.

In the evenings I returned to Elvira, to bird droppings and cackle emanating from six cages of chickadees, finches, cockatoos, and budgies, and, in a cage by himself, presiding, Raa, a majestic gray parrot, cantankerous, looking down on the world with disdain, having no use for the latest intruder—me. Elvira paid me a crown a day to clean the cages of the menagerie, and I stored the gold coins in a cigar box, preparing for flight. When I opened cage doors, four or five pairs of wings sat on my shoulders and arms, fluttered around the kitchen, pecked. Once their homes were spotless, I whistled, the birds whistled back; I filled their feeding pots—they returned behind bars.

The stroke was a thunderbolt; her left arm stopped conducting, her voice became froggy; the tales dried out. I brought chicken soup to her bed, watched it trickle down her chin. She stared with her good eye and shook her head.

"The curse … it is over … all over …."

I patted her immobile arm, told her we'd manage, but knew I could not stay forever, to look after her and the birds.

"My babies … get rid …," she rasped.

I placed ads, sold the finches, gave away the chickadees and the rest, until only the large cage remained.

Raa stared at me as Elvira sat unmoving in front of the window, her radio silent, "Can't bear it anymore." Raa stopped eating; his feathers littered the bottom of the cage; he shrieked his grief. When I let him out of the cage, he pecked at my ear, drawing blood, then sat on the headboard of Elvira's bed.

His caw was unearthly, Wagnerian. "Awake, the dawn is drawing near … a blissful nightingale."

Elvira stretched out her good arm and Raa sat on it. "Twilight, not dawn," she said.

Her voice was clear and firm. "You know what to do …."

I looked at the kitchen counter littered with forks, skewers, knives. My eyes settled on the cleaver, then on Elvira's expectant face.

Thea Swanson

Honey Buzzard

I'm sorry I floated out the door in house sandals with no keys or words or phone, leaving charred rice and your disappointment untended, but I had just heard about the honey buzzard and how it flies a ten-thousand-mile line from South Africa to Finland, avoiding great swaths of water because it knows it can't handle that, so it clings to the edges of solid geography, aware it will tire, that its wings can stretch for only so long, despite its yellow piercing eye, circled by scaled feathers like armor. You see, the world is on fire. And we have this honey buzzard who just wants to get to where she needs to go, but ashy plumes feather the sky, sparked from dry air, ready like yeast. And even if she is able to soar unscathed or maybe just heat-tinged and disoriented or maybe just heavy with grief, even if her yellow eye can still see but is dulled and red-ringed, even if she makes it out alive, I couldn't shake the idea, as our rural roads softened my unsupported ankles mile after mile, leaving you to flounder while I headed toward the pier, hours away and soon to be dark but pulled nevertheless like a magnet, the idea that her wings may give no matter how strong, that she may need to fly downward, busting through a billow, only to be met with gray waves.

Francine Witte

The Day Is a Diamond

The Day Is a Diamond

Light passing through to the infinite. My phone rings. Tomorrow calling. Tells me I am in a boat in a river and don't bother looking for land. Soon enough, tomorrow says, this will all make sense. This is no stranger than anything else tomorrow has promised. I see an island full of caves to disappear in and whooshwillow to lie under. I see a piece of sun in the sky. The hang of light in the air above the island doesn't make anything look faceted, carated. I remind myself how a diamond is made, carbon to pressure to glitter. I remind myself that I should wait.

The Day Is a Ruby

Color of a broken heart. Color of bloodshot eye, no sleep because because. I was a valentine once; I waited for the phone to ring, to beep, to buzz, whatever it does. But it didn't. I waited some more and the waiting became an island where I sat under a blush of tree and hint of moon. I remind myself of the red in my blood, color of a ruby stone, how it gives me life, gives me tomorrow. How sometimes tomorrow is a red lip pout, all memory and promise and none of it true. I remind myself that I shouldn't wait.

The Day Is a Sapphire

Blue cool of another chance. Every morning, every tomorrow is OK, let's try again. It is plump berry in my mother's china. How skin-fragile this tiny bowl is. I could break it like a bone. I pour my coffee into a tea cup, though my mother always said it was wrong.

How wrong it is to tell a tea cup it's wrong. To tell it that's it's only made for tea. I remind myself that I am a blue, unclouded sky, and I will fill myself today with birds and sweet lilac and the sounds from a distant carousel. I remind myself it's time to begin.

The Day Is an Emerald

Green meadows everywhere. I remember play and parks and embroidery cards in Cheryl's backyard. Her father by the barbecue waving away the smoke that rose up around him like a cobra. The day is new and smells of mint and all the things tomorrow promised us yesterday. I think of my friends from when I was small and sprout, how we had a million tomorrows ahead of us. We didn't think about it when Cheryl's father died, sudden and lung-heavy, or when Cheryl and I went our separate ways, how life turns into branches and everyone you ever meet goes off on a different one. I remind myself this is the way life is. I remind myself to take another breath.

Kathryn Silver-Hajo

Bedtime at the Co-Ed, Company-Wide, Team-Building, Social-Bonding, Mosquito-Buzzing, Rain-Sogging Camping Trip in the Woods

Chance placed us side by side at the far end of the five-person tent, colleagues toss-turning, and I'm so near I hear you breathe, smell the soft cotton-sweat musk of you as rain pitapats gentle at first then insistent as rivulets flow, snake nearer, and I move closer, wondering if you feel it, too, drunk though not drunk, feel that calm decorum you've mastered buckle and break, a trick of god, nature, or biology, call it what you will, and somehow we touch, but I'll never know if you rolled into my warmth to escape the tide or from some dark, inexpressible desire.

Evelyn Maguire

Primordial Juice

My boyfriend made me a vitamin C drink. We read online that too much vitamin C could make a period come faster, could work like an organic abortion. The condom broke. I suspected that he could feel it when it broke and decided to keep going anyway. He denied this. The vitamin C drink tasted far worse than orange juice, but I licked the cup clean.

At home, my stepmother was trying to get pregnant with my father's child. "Ouch," she said as he pressed a needle into her butt. "Right in the kicker." How many needles had been stuck in her butt? Hundreds, it seemed like. I didn't think she would be a very good mother. I peeled a clementine for good measure. The white stuff stuck in between my teeth.

They told me they were going out for dinner; they thought I had plans to eat at my boyfriend's. "Plans change," I said. They told me the reservation was only for two.

Leftover noodles, clementine, rocky road ice cream, clementine. I watched a reality show about teenage mothers. There were plenty of other things on, but I made myself watch it. Part penance, part curiosity. The teenage mothers cried very often about how the baby-faced fathers weren't doing what they were supposed to do.

I called my boyfriend. "Hello?" he answered.

"I want you to know that if I'm pregnant, I'm going to slit your throat if you won't change diapers or if you stay out late or if you don't know our baby's blood type."

"OK," he said.

"I mean it. I really mean it."

"I know."

☾

Our science teacher bought a dozen fertilized chicken eggs. They turned orange under a heat lamp. A graveyard of odd tombstones. A mouth full of rounded teeth. There were twelve students in the class. Through a drafting process, we took turns using a sharpie to claim our egg. I got to pick sixth. I chose an egg that looked like all the other eggs.

I drew a clementine slice on the shell. It came out more like a fan.

Birth was all around me. I noticed it everywhere. Our math teacher was swelling like a zit. My neighbor's dog just had a litter. Every news story I read was about why or why not women should be allowed to get cells scraped out of their insides. There were rumors that Sadie the senior was knocked up by Kevin from gym class. Had it always been like this? Or was it like when you learned the meaning behind a new word and then saw it everywhere? Sometimes, when too many things were strange coincidences, I started to re-believe my old childhood nightmare that I was the only real person alive and that everything around me was just a dream my brain had produced.

My boyfriend insisted that he wasn't a figment of my imagination. We sat in the shade of a parking-lot tree. He bought me cherry-flavored water ice, which I slurped without much passion.

"That's exactly what you would say if you were a figment of my imagination," I said. He told me I was impossible. The way he said it sounded like something his mother probably said to his father. For some reason, that made me laugh.

I sat in the guest bathroom, which had a vent on the ceiling that let me listen to what my father and stepmother were saying. I always expected some terrible drama.

Overheard that evening:

"What if we took one of the neighbor's puppies?"

"Puppies and babies make a cute combo."

"Maybe a puppy would be the thing, would be the right omen for the baby."

"I don't think something can be an omen if you make it yourself."

"What would you want to name the puppy?"

"Seymour."

"That's a really good name."

I was part relieved and part disappointed by their mundane conversations.

Still no period. It wasn't yet due, anyway, but I had hoped all the vitamin C would speed me along. Each morning when I picked my boyfriend up for school, he handed me a shaker bottle of vitamin C drink. It was like he was my coach and I was an athlete in training. He asked after my progress. "No blood yet, coach," I'd say.

"Keep up the good work, champ," he'd say back.

In AP psychology, I read forums about whether or not a guy could feel if a condom broke. The answers were split based on gender. I supposed that made sense. Though maybe it was a great male conspiracy to lie about feeling the condom break. Kind of like the great female conspiracy about faking it. Except the male lie was in pursuit of male pleasure, and the female lie was also in pursuit of male pleasure. This theory made me furious at my boyfriend, who texted me, "WTF??" after I told him to get his own ride home.

My cell phone rang and rang that evening. I left it in the kitchen. My dad came into my room.

"Why not give the kid a break?" he said. "He sounds upset."

"I want him to be upset. Women have been upset for *centuries*!"

My dad made the face he was taught in family therapy after my mom died to signal he was "listening."

At school, we practiced turning the chicken eggs. Turning was apparently an important part of egg care so that the developing chick didn't get stuck to the shell. The thought made me queasy, and then I worried that being queasy meant I was pregnant. Every possible bodily feeling could mean you were pregnant, according to the internet. Throwing up? Pregnant. Aching? Pregnant. Sad? Pregnant. Tired? Pregnant. Hungry? Not Hungry? Bloating? Cramping? Pregnant, pregnant, pregnant, pregnant.

When I was fifteen, I tore a muscle in my back while playing soccer. The doctor asked if I could be pregnant. I told him I had never had sex. He made me take a test anyway. The muscle tear could affect the baby, he told me. What baby? I wanted to scream. The test was obviously negative. I started crying for no real reason.

I flipped my egg over so that the clementine was upside-down and a question-mark was right-side-up. I shared my egg with someone in the sixth-period class, the question-mark-drawer. We shared so that the egg would be flipped a few times a day. I wondered if my egg's other parent was a boy. Not that it mattered.

When I got home, my boyfriend was waiting on my porch with a vitamin C drink. One of his knees was scraped up, but I made a point of not asking what happened. I took the shaker bottle from him and started to drink. He told me he really couldn't feel the condom breaking. He swore on his mother's life. But, I knew that he didn't like his mother that much, so I was unsure how to take that.

Deep down, I think I believed him. But, I also really didn't want to believe him, because then I wouldn't have anywhere to put all the anger inside of me. Where would it go? A red fog suffocating me day and night. He asked if he could stay for dinner at my house. His parents were working late, and his mother had left him cold eggplant parm, which he hated.

"Why don't you go buy a pregnancy test?" I asked him instead of answering.

"Isn't it too early to tell?"

"Maybe."

"My cousin works at the CVS, anyway."

"Rick?"

"No, Marcia."

"Oh. You could borrow my car and drive to the one in Englewood."

"Why don't *you* drive your *own* car to Englewood?"

Furious all over again, I told him he should be thankful that his mother was even alive and to enjoy her cold eggplant parm.

My stepmother got her period. Dinner was very solemn. I was stewing in envy. And also a secret relief that was being beaten up by my guilty conscience. I didn't want them to have a baby, but I knew that feeling was morally wrong and so I tried not to feel it. When half my stepmother's tofu steak was gone, she got up and poured herself a fishbowl-sized glass of wine. Her backwash made minnows.

"We might get a puppy," my dad said to me, something green on his lip. "Wouldn't that be exciting?"

I wished that I had let my boyfriend stay for dinner. He was very good at having conversations with my dad, who for some reason spoke to my boyfriend like he was an adult and to me like a slow child. I wondered if I was pregnant, would my parents want to raise it like my sibling, and would we all pretend that's how it really happened, like what happened to Ted Bundy?

"Did you guys know that Ted Bundy was raised to think his mother was his sister?" I asked. "Do you think that's why he wanted to kill women?"

"Can't we ever talk about something nice?" my dad said.

My stepmother drank her fishbowl wine. "All men secretly hate women to some degree," she said. "Don't you secretly hate all men? At least a little?"

"Hey, now," my dad said.

I thought about that while I chewed my tofu steak. "Yes," I decided. "I guess I do."

She nodded. "That's why the lesbians are so much happier than us."

After dinner, I stayed up late reading "Am I Pregnant?" forums on the Internet. I read a horrifying story about a girl in her first year of college who didn't know she was pregnant until what she took to be terrible food poisoning from shrimp tacos turned into a baby in the toilet. I wanted to throw up. It seemed that there was no escape from the uncanny mystique of the female body.

I texted my boyfriend: "Do you ever feel afraid of your own body?"

His reply buzzed a few minutes later: "I am sometimes afraid of my mind. Not body."

That made no sense to me and furthered my theory that my boyfriend and I would never understand one another.

The eggs were close to hatching. When we shone a flashlight at the shells, we could see the chicks' bodies inside. I looked at my clementine chick. It looked like all the other ones but felt more special. "Good job, little guy," I whispered to it. "Keep growing."

My period was one day late.

During gym-class field hockey, I shoved my shoulders and elbows into my classmates. I made them mad, felt heady when they hit me back. I angled my stomach towards their pointed limbs. Every hit felt promising. My body was a dam ready to burst, ready to flood its tributaries, its deltas, its creeks. I could imagine it so clearly. But, in the bathroom, no blood.

"So?" my boyfriend asked on the way to AP psychology.

"Might have to prep the coat hanger, coach," I said.

"That's not funny," he said.

"I'm the one who gets to decide what's funny or not."

Overheard vent conversation that evening:

Stepmother: "What if it never works?"

Dad: "We have to keep a positive outlook."

Stepmother: "It's easier for you; you *have* a child."

When my period was two days late, my boyfriend and I went to a party at our friend Ozzy's house. I mixed vitamin C powder in with my beer. "That's disgusting," Ozzy said.

"I have a cold," I told him. The house was hot, moisture from dancing and drinking bodies condensed on the windows. I lost my boyfriend sometime after the third round of stack cup and went outside to cool down.

Ozzy's older cousin Rebecca, who I knew of via Facebook but had never met, was smoking weed on a lawn chair in the backyard. I sat in the plastic chair next to her. Mosquitos investigated my ankles. When Rebecca offered the joint to me, I accepted. I held the subsequent burning urge to cough inside of me until it passed.

I asked Rebecca if she thought what my stepmother had said about men hating women and women hating men was true.

Rebecca was very wise with her smoldering joint and her slicked-back bun and her small earrings. She exhaled smoke through her nose like a dragon. "I think that question is very heteronormative," she said, "and is a line of inquiry that further solidifies the gender binary rather than helping to dismantle it."

"OK," I said. "But do you think guys can feel when a condom breaks?"

She tapped the ash. "Definitely."

When I opened the door to my house after school, a puppy ran out. A brown-and-white fluffy thing on stubby legs, it tumbled over itself and over my feet and over the step. I brought the wriggling puppy back inside, where my dad and stepmom were laughing. They seemed to expect me to be beside myself with happiness at this not-surprising turn of events, so I made my face smile as hard as it could.

"His name's Seymour!" my stepmother announced. For the first time in weeks, her face looked not depressed.

"Isn't he just great?" My dad ruffled the puppy's head, seemingly unbothered when Seymour started to chew on his fingers.

"So cute," I agreed, still smiling hard. "Seymour is the perfect name."

"One happy family," my dad said.

Later, potato-sized Seymour lay asleep in my arms while my dad stuck the nightly needle in her butt. I imagined a scenario in which a witch came to the house and offered my parents a deal: Sacrifice Seymour in exchange for a human baby. Would they take the deal? It was a stupid hypothetical because I knew the answer for sure. I patted Seymour's sleeping head while my dad swabbed my stepmother's butt with an alcohol wipe.

And what if the deal was for me instead? Would they trade me in for a new baby? I knew that was a childish thought, but I couldn't stop thinking it.

I looked up abortion clinics on my laptop late at night. The closest one was three hours away. Since I was being proactive, I would only have to take a pill and then bleed profusely for 24 hours, and then I wouldn't be pregnant anymore. The thought of telling my stepmother that I was pregnant while she was not made me want to vomit. What did it mean in the grand scheme of life and the universe and the morally good and the morally wrong that I could get pregnant from one instance of a half-torn condom at the age of sixteen and my forty-year-old stepmother couldn't get pregnant despite all the medical help that an upper-middle-class income could buy? In what world, divinely created or otherwise, was a sixteen-year-old decreed more apt to raise a child than a forty-year-old?

On the abortion clinic's website, advertisements popped up for a 100 percent organic cotton sling to hold a baby close to your chest.

☾

When my period was four days late, I pretended to leave for school but drove back home once my dad and stepmother had gone to work. I had been ignoring my boyfriend since talking to Rebecca at the party. I thought I would maybe break up with him but wanted to wait until I knew if I would need him to chip in for an abortion or not. Seymour was in the backyard and licked my hand when I held it out.

I went upstairs to look in the cabinets of my parents' bathroom. As I had hoped, I found a handful of pregnancy tests behind the rolls of toilet paper. Would she notice one missing? I assumed she wouldn't, so addled by hormones and disappointments, and then felt bad for such an unkind assumption. I took a test anyway.

But, when it came time to pee on it, I couldn't do it. At the last moment, right as the pee was about to hit the stick and reveal the secrets of my body that somehow this plastic test could understand though my brain could not, I moved it out of the way. I wrapped it back up and put it in my backpack for later. Maybe my period would come on the way to school.

Sadie the senior was, in fact, pregnant. Whether or not the father was Kevin from gym class remained unconfirmed, though he did look pale while we did our warm-up stretches. I took Sadie's pregnancy as a good omen—surely, there couldn't be *two* knocked-up girls at Unionville High. What were the odds?

Everyone was talking about Sadie. She was so brave for posting about it on Instagram, she was a slut and it was just a matter of time, she was going to get it aborted, she had tried to get it aborted and it failed, her parents wouldn't let her get it aborted, her parents were going to throw it out *unless* she got it aborted, and hey, weren't her boobs way bigger now?

I tried not to join in, being in my own pregnancy limbo as I was, but it was hard not to speculate. When she walked down the hallway, the school was silent.

Overheard vent conversation that evening:

"Maybe this is just how it's going to be. Not everyone gets everything they want. Most people don't get even a little bit of what they want."

Silence. Just when I was about to give up and get off the toilet—
"If I can't be a mother, I think I might die."

The eggs started to hatch. The students in the sixth-period class were notified via a crackling intercom announcement and invited to join us for the birth of our chicks. Pair by pair, our class identified their mystery sixth-period co-parent. My co-parent, the question-mark-drawer, turned out to be Lucy Pham. It seemed, based on the couple pairings, that our science teacher had taken pains to present as diverse an array of parental pairs as possible. The only thing I knew about Lucy Pham was that she had worn the same puka-shell necklace every day since her family's trip to Hawaii in the fourth grade.

Together, Lucy and I watched a tiny, sharp beak push through our shared egg. Over and over, the chick pushed against the shell, ever so slowly leaving its world to enter ours. When its full head emerged for the first time, I looked over to Lucy and saw that she was crying. Watching her cry made me cry. Side by side, we sniffled as our chick birthed itself.

After science class, I discovered that my boyfriend had stuck a yellow flower in the vent of my locker. The stem snapped when I yanked it out.

I waited for him after AP psychology. "You could've just said sorry," I said. I dropped the yellow flower at his feet. "You *should* say sorry." He stuck his hands into the stupid pockets of his stupid ugly hoodie. "Say you're fucking sorry!"

"I'm sorry," he said. He looked very serious. "I'm sorry. I'm sorry. I'm sorry."

Richard Newman

Three Little Backyard Songs

1.
A small murder of crows attacks a kitten
while my son watches, scared but fascinated.
A hungry stray dog, badly scratched and bitten,
stares from the woods as crows attack the kitten
and hopes for scraps, the laws of nature written
in stones we throw at the birds, but it is fated.
The growing number of crows murders the kitten
as my son watches, scared but fascinated.

2.
Young jackdaws who can't walk or fly
try not to move in our backyard—
cat food. From shadows, stray cats eye
young jackdaws who can't walk or fly.
The fledglings learn to fly or die.
The parents shriek and try to guard
young jackdaws who can't walk or fly
while nothing moves in my backyard.

3.
The creatures who can't fly or flee
must learn to live here on the ground.
A kitten stalks beneath a tree
the jackdaws who can't fly or flee
while crows strike kittens from all around.
Blood, feathers, fur—nature's decree.
We creatures who can't fly or flee
must learn to live here on the ground.

Cat Dixon

For Carolyn

You don't belong here. You belong to the air, to North
Carolina, to California, to the first strings who practice
hard, to the card players who never fold, to follies, to Eden
where the trees are evergreen, to the indelicate candidate
skidding to the edge of a five-story building, to Lake
Superior, to ambrosia, to Gate 52, to the better life not
promised to you, to the pontoon boot for the flood's
coming, to the screen door that slams, to the roulette
wheel with its little white ball, to the somersault
of a gymnast, to the difference between night
and day, to every single word in the fifty-two-page
script, to the midnight sky full of stars.

Michael Brasier

The Air Burns When I Breathe

Plumes of smoke
        from Catlettsburg steel pillars
                Enter West Virginia, roads under construction

orange witch hats and blacktop cavities
        patches of freshly dried concrete
                unbalanced even on the drivable parts

Construction zones, reduce to fifty-five,
        but long trips over cracked and crippled
                highways don't deserve outstanding tickets

yet there is nowhere for miles
        where the shoulder isn't tattered
                with travelers' remnants and tire shreds

from the trucker brotherhood, the interstate
        closed, chains dragging a semi out of the road
                one less traveler on the impaired highway

                one more plume of smoke

Anita Vijayakumar

Connecting at the Clinic

We met at the county fairgrounds ten miles from my house. It had been converted into a massive vaccine clinic. The horse stalls were removed, the bales of hay scattered outside. One vaccinator and one data collector per team; other than that, the assignments were random. We started out with awkward small talk that evolved quickly. You were in marketing; I was a psychiatrist. You worked for a large firm. I'd just shuttered my practice due to my spouse's job shift. I missed the soft humility of helping patients.

We found joy and purpose administering COVID vaccines in those early days, back when people scrambled to get on waitlists and stood outside pharmacy doors after closing for the dredges of the vial. Through car windows, we took medical histories and poked shivering arms with thin needles.

In the exhaust-filled moments during vehicle transitions, we chatted about our lives. As kids, we both collected scratch-and-sniff stickers, both preferred ice cream over cake. Our abusive childhoods matched. We went to the same college, just a couple years apart. We both had three kids. My social anxiety didn't put you off; your stutter didn't confuse me.

Shyly, I envisioned our friendship blossoming. Meeting up for coffee, clinking glasses of chardonnay at book clubs where everyone read the book. I saw the hunger for friendship in your stance, as I imagine you saw it in mine.

Just as I pulled out my phone for your number, you asked, "What country were you born in?" My fingers stopped. Not you, too. You saw your question as curiosity, not an act of privilege or microaggression. Apparently my history was not enough to manifest belonging. To you, I was still an "other."

Close your eyes. Listen. We sound the same, don't we? The same elongated A when we say "vaccine," the same wheesh of loyalty when we talk about the Cubs. Now open them. My skin is brown, my eyes black. And you: white skin, blue eyes. You were born in a Chicago hospital room fifteen miles south of here, tethering you to this country with rope as strong as purest silk. And I, my friend, was born on the very same floor, just right next door.

Kirby Wright

The Widow Hunts

Wendy Adams was prone to crushes because she was lonely, a loneliness veering toward desperation during the holidays. Two years had passed since she'd had a fling with a Bellagio acrobat in Vegas. Her secret desire was to make out with John Elway. She imagined him nibbling her breasts with his full lips and wolfish teeth.

I usually cross paths with Wendy at department Christmas parties; 2022 is no exception. I spot her sashaying in a little black dress. There's a pewter chain around her neck and she has a model's strut. She turns a cheek to me, inviting a peck. I peck. My salami lips leave a grease spot on her foundation. I ramble on about literature, favorite authors and applying for a guest lecture spot at Trinity College Dublin. Her vivacious green eyes turn dull, making her look old.

"What's the last book you read?" she quizzes.

"*Black Like Me.*"

"Read that during Woodstock," she smirks.

Wendy brags about being photographed as "the Colorado blond" in Osaka while posing with local doctors at a seafood restaurant. She was in Japan attending her husband's lectures on cutting-edge treatments for third-degree burns.

"They served whitefish," she tells me, "which I flat-out refused."

"They serve you the whole fish?" I asked.

"Head to tail. Even my man passed," she said, "and he was a fanatic for Asian cuisine."

Wendy's forehead, brow, and eyes have zero wrinkles. Botox? She keeps her white-blond hair shoulder length. Her perfume smells of flowers, yellow roses, I think. I suppose she's attractive, but I remind myself I'm taken after swallowing a cream cheese hors d'oeuvre.

Wendy's man committed suicide after failing to deliver the required research for a federal grant; he spent the entire million on solo global travel, luxury hotels, and sports cars, while Wendy slaved in CSU's nursing department. Her loss blew holes through heart and pocketbook. The feds attached the Del Mar mansion, but she paid off the debt within seven years. She has LA Chargers season tickets. It's a game she got hooked on with her husband. She cheers and shouts with the usual gang of beer-drunk men, her soprano voice rising above their deep chorus into the lights.

Jenny Stalter

Beginnings

I still have my key, the one you gave me when you asked me to be your hunk, a hunk of burning love, because I was singing top-volume with Elvis. You shut it off and told me to keep going; I want to hear only your voice, Janie. I don't miss you. I'm totally over you. I'm just here to get my Jenny Saville print, the one you said I should buy because the woman looks like me with my thick thighs and heavy breasts and pink skin. I just lied. Now I wonder if you suggested the Saville for its grotesquerie, like you were beginning to see the fractures inside me.

Your apartment smells the way I remember but with something else. Something woody. Spicy. Sort of masculine, almost. I grab the Saville, and then I think to look for the flamingo flower I gave you for our anniversary, because you never watered it. But, I don't see it.

I look in the bathroom. You're still leaving your wadded scrubs on the bathroom floor by the shower, even though the hamper is right outside the door. I remember the first time I saw you wearing those scrubs. You were nursing at the clinic. I told the doctor I didn't want the pain meds, that I just wanted it done. So, you took my hand and held it like a child's. Your voice was reassuring and soft, like sliding on something warm. To distract me, you asked what kind of music I liked, and I said Frog Eyes, and the sound went schhhhhhh, and I said Silver Jews, and you smiled down at me and said you like Frog Eyes, too, and the doctor told you she was going around my uterus one more time to make sure she got it all out. You already felt like home. The softness of woman after a man. I gave you my number that day. Later, you would tell me I didn't deserve the pain, that I should have taken the meds, that I didn't have to punish myself for getting rid of it. I wasn't punishing myself, and it didn't hurt. I got some cramps, and it was finally over with Miguel. A beginning. Now, seeing her monogrammed towel on the rack next to yours—that's what hurts.

I find a collage frame loaded with pictures of you and Sonya, a ridiculous inspirational quote in the center. The kind of hacky, saccharine shit we used to make fun of. I get queasy. Something precarious folds then breaks inside me. I'm surrounded by new, different plants, ones I can't identify. Huge, looming, confrontational ones. Squat, adorable blossoms on the windowsill. Some extra-long crawling thing hooked to the entire living-room ceiling, green and waxy and winking, a watch-me-thrive kind of wink. A fuck-you kind of wink. The bitch is terraforming. I don't like calling women bitches, so I take it back. Sonya is terraforming.

She is a snake. Her name even sounds like snakes. Sssssssonya. I know because I go through the pictures on your laptop and find the ones of you both cooking in your underwear, flamingo flower photobombing the background. When we were still together. When the color for me was bleeding away from your eyes. When you told me to stop singing with Carey Mercer, because it was nice to just hear the fucking song. I head to the bedroom. Maybe I'm punishing myself for losing you.

There's a multifauna duvet cover I've never seen crumpled at the foot of the bed. The harness is black on the exposed white sheet, like a beetle belly-up on a buttercream cake. We never used a strap-on, so I know it's hers. I get on my knees in the bed where you loved me, and I pretend I'm you, mimicking how you sound, how you move your hips when you're close. I say, I love you, Janie, out loud, the way you did the first time and for five years after that. The way you did after we harvested purple hyssop to infuse with honey. We barely made it to the bed, your fingers and tongue tracing the honey across my lips. We stickied the sheets and our hair, warming the air with the scent of ourselves and hyssop's smell of fresh licorice. I wipe my tears and snot on your pillow when I'm done. I breathe deep, in search of myself, but it just smells like a detergent I don't know.

I slip into the harness and strap it on. I walk to the kitchen to make a sandwich. I pretend I'm Sonya, dick swinging around, confident you're mine. My love.

I open the window to the alley, tonguing gluten-free bread off the roof of my mouth (when did you start eating this shit?). Some kids are painting bubble throw-ups on the brick building next door. I stand here, more grotesque than any painting, with the alien weight of your new life bobbing between my thighs. I'm me again and I know I need to let you go. I unstrap and throw first the dildo and then the key out the window—another beginning. It's as painful as a birth. You'll be home from work soon. Before I go, I press my hand to the glass, leaving a print.

Patricia Q. Bidar

Are You Experienced?

It's Wednesday,

Conversano's day for Cabrillo Avenue, on the east side of the town. Near I-10 across from the Little League field and the refinery.

His Wednesday boy lives on a cul-du-sac. Conversano parks around the corner and strolls to his student's home. His uncased guitar is strapped to his back. He wears his customary ivory turtleneck shirt under a sport coat. He carries his briefcase, which is stuffed with sheet music. Conversano smokes the stub-end of a cigar, channeling a bee-bop backdrop. There's a jazzy snap to his walk.

A tanned mom in a pink bikini washes her car. She gives him her usual tight smile. Conversano will spend most of the lesson thinking of her tawny stomach.

A haggard man about Conversano's age locks his battered work truck and carries his lunch bucket into his house. Poor sap. The screen door bangs behind him, releasing the smell of tomato, oregano, and garlic.

In front of the Wednesday boy's home, Conversano flicks his stogie butt into the gutter. Before he has a chance to knock, the mother, a shapeless redhead, smiles and leads him to the television room.

She has told him she enjoys singing, and that she follows a late-night guitar lesson show on KCET. An odd thing to tell a guitar teacher she has hired for her son. He doesn't know how to read the look in her eyes; is it hope he'll offer a discount, or something more? He has no feeling for a square like her. She has also said that her husband works graveyard at Todd Shipyard. A day sleeper. It explains the aluminum foil covering the upstairs corner windows.

The boy waits in the family room on a kitchen chair, guitar in his lap. He is dressed in vertically striped pants and a stamped leather belt. A Hang Ten T-shirt with its embroidered bare feet. A shy boy. He's asked to learn Django Reinhardt, but Conversano said they would start with something even cooler.

The Peter Max wallpaper and wall of books. The row of bowling trophies—apparently, the boy's father had almost gone semi-pro. The squawking cockatiel in its cage.

"Man, the first unrainy day here in unrainy LA," he says in greeting.

The Boy

nods. Even though he is only ten years old, he is already taller than compact Mr. Conversano, who always stands during lessons. He likes this about his teacher, who has lived in New York and once appeared as an extra in a movie. Even the teacher's sour breath, the white flakes on the shoulders of his jacket, do not subtract from the teacher's glamor.

He is a helpful boy; all his teachers say so. He gets the metronome started and launches into the chords of the song he is learning: "Foxy Lady" by Jimi Hendrix. This time Mr. Conversano does something he has never done before: He begins to sing along. He delivers "Foxy" with Hendrix's whispered urgency.

"Again?" the boy asks when they are done. And Mr. Conversano nods. He begins the song again and wonder of wonders: his mother's voice penetrates the hollow-core door of the family room. The two adults are singing together, *Down on the scene. Wanna get up and scream.*

Foxee.

The boy daydreams of such things happening. Choreographed fantasias. Day-Glo colors and whirling dresses. Dashing men in suit jackets, redolant of cocktails and cigars. Women with white teeth and wide, glossy smiles. The boy's father smokes pot and grows his hair past his ears. The Aqua Velva the boy gave him for Christmas has never been touched.

The boy continues playing. The metronome tock-tock-tocks. "Cha-cha-cha!" Mr. Conversano adds when the song is done. That's a good one. The boy hunches over his guitar to hide his smile. The bird, Toulouse, emits an especially loud squawk.

"One more tiiime!" the teacher says.

The mother's breasts
are pressed against the family room door. Mr. Conversano is the reason she dons her dancing shoes every Wednesday at four. Puts on lipstick. The smell of Mr. Conversano's cologne brings her back to her single years, working for the Los Angeles Unified School District offices downtown. The swish of her stockings as she walked to her building from the bus stop. The feel of her cashmere sweater; she'd bought one for herself every month with her paycheck. The rest, she gave to her mother. Her hair was platinum blond back then. She'd idolized Kim Novak's look, Billie Holliday's voice.

She yearns to access one of those old sweaters and pretty bras without waking her husband, upstairs in their stifling bedroom. Her breasts and belly are heavy and soft. She eats goods from the nearby discount bakery before the television every night. The guitar teacher's voice, the scents he brings into the house, carry her through her week. The mother snaps her fingers as she sings.

And now they are dancing
in the shadow of the refinery and the Vincent Thomas Bridge. They trip the light fantastic under spotlights spilling pools onto the shining lanes of the Bowl Lotta Love Lanes, out near the fishing landing.

Mr. Conversano, the Wednesday boy, the heavyset mama. The blinking, chest-scratching father. The bikini'd neighbor, now in a bathing costume like Esther Williams in *Neptune's Daughter*. A way-out version of "Are You Experienced?" wails, with his mom on bongos—Mr. Conversano, obviously, on electric guitar.

The rest of them—the lunch-bucket dad, the school principal, the Navy Housing kids who called the boy *Pee Pants* and *Twinkletoes* at school—raise bare arms in feathered formation, with the boy in the center lane. Now they are lifting the boy, turning in formation and bearing him high atop their heads.

And now setting him down onto the honeyed lane, where his ball awaits. Everyone with shining eyes and bright smiles as the boy throws *Bam! Bam! BAM!* nothing but strikes.

JW Burns

In Search of Lost Country Vegetables

The label on the can reads "Chicken Soup With Country Vegetables."

Vegetables: potatoes, carrots, peas, beans, celery, tomato plus various oils, extracts, powders; Country, a distinct modifier for an ethereal phenomenon. Given proper light, moisture, a reasonable temperature range, and appropriate fertilizer, vegetables will grow practically anywhere. No need for a rural setting. I had an acquaintance who grew all the varieties above and more in a small vacant space located in the heart of a vibrating urban area. City vegetables fingerprint the eye and the appetite much the same as country vegetables, seeds, dry roots, the common miracle sustaining sprout, branch, bud, flower, fruit or underground burial/renewal come to life. So in our wretchful visions we know that the veggies in the can were agribusiness grown; produced on value-chain links enhanced by mechanized farming, chemical fertilizers, and pesticides and sustained by the profit motive. Flavor and, in some cases, food value sacrificed on the altar of a larger, more durable product. Of course there ain't 'nough room on the label to explain all this, and I doubt soup manufacturers would want to stream such candor in any case.

On a superficially blighted bit of land behind a towering condo complex, the aforementioned urban farmer planted his garden in the derelict chassis of an old Chevy; expanding his reach, the battered frame became the centerpiece of a living, shifting composition strung with a flurry of string, wire, conduit containers, wicks, waterpipes, a whole hydroponic sanctuary in addition to the cultivated soil underneath, from which spouted slower growing plants. The gods of agriculture were well pleased, supplied sun, rain, bubble-blown evenings wherein we gathered, eating, drinking, settling on lounge chairs to savor a newfound attachment to credulous life within the citified landscape.

According to the wealth of accumulated knowledge concerning the evolution of life on Earth which some would exclude from human circulation, vegetables got their start as modestly mild wildlife forms, small green leaves, purple stalks, tiny endearing fruits clinging to a quirky vine through often terrifying macroclimatic events. The photosynthesizing stubble contributing to the oxygen count, initial tentative presence symbolically joined with more mobile life to flourish, in many ways plant life remaining on the same beginning rungs of the ladder of being. Another thankful tool assisting those evolving hominids in their often-unlikely survivalist climb—allowing edible plant matter to provide basic sustenance. To be eaten rather than glorified: Few people grow okra or squash for their magnificent floral outbursts.

The yeoman farmer, though continuously displaced through U.S. history, has maintained a positive mythic hold on the American imagination. Now more or less shorn of his historical fleece the tiller of the soil has yet retained certain sentimental attachments to fill out our colossal self-depiction: honesty, rugged independence, good health, noncommercial devotion to the land, life as a kind of simple joy, these themes raised up along with pole beans and leeks. No matter that the countryside has in many cases lost its virtuous way: commercial agribusiness gulping land and market, meth trailers behind the crumbling barn, semi-ghost villages dangling from bumpy two-lane roads to nowhere, derelict farmhouses, all this weaving a tattered tapestry across the agrarian landscape.

Daughters of a long-ago strain of commonsense supernaturalism, two sisters flourished in their own manner. During many years in the century preceding this one, they lived in Virginia approximately thirty-five miles from one another. Lanier dwelled in the city, Annie on a country farm. Both planted, tended and harvested vegetable garden plots for primarily family consumption, although both did sell some produce, Lanier to neighbors, Annie to those frequenting a weekly farmer's market. Garden surplus was periodically canned for future use by the sisters themselves, taking advantage of a policy by the local cannery that allowed small tract growers to process their fruits and vegetables at the facility, providing materials, chopping and blanching stations, and the canning run itself for a reasonable fee.

Grandson to one and grandnephew to the other, with a child's lazily distracted involvement, my small helping hands were twisted to the enterprise, everything from preparing the ground for planting to hectic mornings at the cannery. And there was some sort of innate warmth in participating in the labors of the two women, although at the time I didn't give a fart in a hurricane about vegetables, nutritional eating, how old women worked the earth, embroidered growth as a spiritual undertaking, the charm of including a guardian angel in every potential bite. But in the process I learned to eat and enjoy my vegetables—most of them, anyway—which I'm sure has stood me in good stead, aiding in counteracting bad habits conjured during those years following my gardening experiences when being cool tickled my aqueous humor and tarted those cogent synapses. Of course, without bad habits life wouldn't have been worth living, and I sure as hell wouldn't have survived the tedium to make it to the point of savoring my veggies today.

Country vegetables. Dirt turned, returned, worked fertilized with chicken shit, manure from the same cows, mules, horses, lightly mulched with straw, weeded by hand hoe, watered from a hose when needed, no pesticides or antifungals other than an odorous mixture made with natural ingredients. The vegetables themselves when loaded together for the cannery mixing quite amicably, likewise following their transition and descent into cans. And my arms, legs, back, fingers aching, pricked, smeared, stained and functionally acclaimed from planting, tending, picking, shelling, husking, chopping, etc.

City agri-industry vegetables. Open the can today and hey, hey! Pour into a saucepan, stir, wait five minutes or less, pour some into a bowl, take up a spoon, scoop, blow, find your quivering mouth, slurp, chew … what you experience somewhat distant from last century's vegetables: carrots muttering pocked half-syllables instead of speaking distinctly; peas slogging through a swamp rather than bursting into a mountainside sunrise; where are potatoes firm and white as a snow-covered landscape, celery crunching boots across the ice, beans afloat on a pristine river, sweet corn smiling teeth ready to inhale the laughter … but this agri-sludge is quick, easy, enflamed with the label, endowed by mass mindset, which is balance gone flat as a dime. Thomas Jefferson holds his can of country vegetable soup under the electric can opener, presses down his rugged individualist index finger, contemplates floating institutionalized profit while straddling the rungs of fiduciary finagling.

It happened without design. My appetite for vegetables didn't so much unravel as disappear along with the vegetables I no longer easily encountered. In their place: fast food; meat swooned between deadweight buns, some dairy, sugar, fat in various guises. Came the occasional daymares and nightfrights typical of a poor diet. Serious only in their cumulative effect. A rogue diet doesn't usually manifest itself in questionable health right away, especially if the imperfect eater is relatively young. Just because ultimately the devil is in the pudding doesn't necessarily translate that angelic transgressiveness abandons the consuming entity all at once. Over time, though, like as not material input will have its way.

During this period I belittled food. Cold or hot, it was something to put in my mouth, chew if required, swallow. Appetite wasn't given an opportunity to assert itself. There was no constructive hunger, maybe just a few piddling hunger pangs rapidly subsumed by synthetic imbalance—cheeseburgers/fries/soda. Taste, torched in abstract skirmishes, left a mouthful of sticky ashes. Swinging through an indigestive wilderness spiked with nausea, acid reflux, headaches, constipation, fatigue … gradually learning that the stomach and intestines are a milieu much greater than the mouth and attendant passage to the former. Easy to please the head both material and spiritual—not necessarily as easy to console the complex gut.

The will to survive pledges not inconsiderable allegiance to the exercise of one's intuition—intuition, contrary to popular wisdom differing from individual to individual—and my gradual return to the consumption of vegetables was urged along by a sense of positive regression to a time when yeoman farmers planted and harvested their modest plots upholding the moral and civic ventures of American democracy, proud, happy, celebrating the miracle of the earth, the simple wealth inherent in cultivating the crops which drive human life to reproduce itself, to prosper and flourish. Or perhaps it was just that a largely vegetarian diet makes me feel better, a me intuitively courting moments held together by inner workings, deviating from the inside out rather than influenced by the outside in. Light makes up maybe 0.005 percent of the universe, water even less. So anything utilizing light and water as primary ingredients to survival and growth must be grit-approved bone-deep slippery yearning for that longshot steady heartbeat clinging to eternity.

Marci Rae Johnson

Litany for the Garden and Its Departed Bamboo

When the world's smallest antelope
visits your garden, it's the hottest part

of the day. She's looking for shade, finally,
after this long journey from desert

to desert, from the isolated place
along the water where trees

can't grow taller than your eyes looking out
from where you sit in your chair on the deck.

Here beside the pond, small mercy
of fern. Cool leaves of the Japanese maple

you planted with your own hands after
the bamboo died and returned,

earth to earth.

Ancient ginkgo, crab apple, pine—
she would say their names in her mind.

Say their names. Locust,
white oak, hawthorn, the purple

redbud in spring before anything else begins.

But something else is beginning now, perhaps,
as she stretches her neck to drink—

the frog unmoving, fish
unafraid, they keep looking out

and out now as the sun touches
its fingertips, tentative, to the stone.

Marci Rae Johnson

Exodus

You have circled this mountain long enough.
Now turn north.

Deuteronomy 2:3

This is the story. For twenty years
you wandered in the wilderness.

The trees were brown. The sand,
the dirt, the watermelon mountain

that turned red only at sunset.
But the blue in your eyes

still a lake, a memory. Remember:
the silence of the wind without trees.

The clouds that never rained.
The woman in your bed

who turned away in the night,
her back a wall. Still,

the offering you burned in the desert:
your eye finding color in the way

the saints in worship took flight
over a green world, a yellow sky,

and beside your bed a map
of the lake you longed for.

Exodus

Now we stand at the water's edge,
the sky a baptism of snow, and rain,

your lips on mine. For twenty years
we wandered alone. Now this lake,
a home.

Patrick Wilcox

Look! The Scrawny Kid Is Crying Again

Look at the playground, at the scrawny kid
laid out on the blacktop trying to understand
his broken nose and all the blood it lets loose

into fevered rain, how so much blood
can let loose from someone, even a kid, and not
kill them. They were kids thrumming with laughter

until they weren't. A halo of wide eyes
and so much blood, but they couldn't die,
not even if they wanted to. Look at the parking lot,

at the scrawny kid now in his car, trying to understand
the procedure and all the rain it lets loose
into fevered love. Look at you in the clinic

trying to understand the halo of wide eyes
and how one moment collapses
into another. You were kids thrumming

with trespass until you weren't. He said he would
be there with you when he knew he couldn't. Rain
collapsed onto the blacktop. Rain never fell

so reckless-hopeful. He wanted to be there
with you trying to understand beginnings
and endings. Rain never fell so warm. He told you

he would be there with you. You had the procedure,
          got in the car, body soaked with novocaine, and agreed
to call it the procedure. Look at him. He has started

          a poem he knows he can't finish. Numb body, numb
sky, numb trespass, numb kid thrumming with hope
          and guilt he knows nothing about. Look at the rain,

at its relentless collapse, relentless poems collapsing,
          sometimes here, sometimes there, how the rain never
ends, not even for a moment, like it doesn't know how.

Matt Gulley

Cigarette Break

Two days before Christmas
I saw a crown of white birds

atop a rusted-brick apartment building
pick up and descend all at once,
unprovoked

and for a moment of obliterative white
anxiety

it was like the whole building was
collapsing
but I gathered myself and had to remember:

the building is still there
and
the foundation is strong.

Contributors' Notes

Katy Aisenberg's poems have recently appeared in *Carve*, *ONE ART*, and other journals. She practices psychology in Cambridge, Massachusetts.

Mikki Aronoff's work appears in *New World Writing Quarterly*, *MacQueen's Quinterly*, *Tiny Molecules*, *Gone Lawn*, *The Citron Review*, and elsewhere. She has received Pushcart Prize, Best of the Net, Best Small Fictions, Best American Short Stories, and Best Microfiction nominations.

Matt Barrett holds an Master of Fine Arts in creative writing (fiction) from the University of North Carolina at Greensboro, and his stories have appeared or are forthcoming in *The Sun*, *The Threepenny Review*, *Baltimore Review*, *SmokeLong Quarterly*, *Best Microfiction 2022* and *Best Microfiction 2023*, *Best Small Fictions 2023*, and more. He teaches creative writing at Gettysburg College and lives in central Pennsylvania with his wife and two kids.

Patricia Q. Bidar is an alum of the University of California, Davis Graduate Writing Program, and also holds a degree in filmmaking. Her work has been included in numerous journals and anthologies, including *Flash Fiction America* (W.W. Norton, 2023), *Best Small Fictions 2023*, and *Best Microfiction 2023*. Her book of short fiction, *Pardon Me for Moonwalking*, will be published by Unsolicited Press in 2025. She lives outside of Oakland, California.

Michael Brasier is a writer born and raised in the Missouri Ozarks. His fiction and poetry have appeared in journals such as *Crack the Spine* and *The Phoenix* and also in the anthology *Paddle Shots*, compiled by the River Pretty Arts Foundation. He works as a copy-and-content editor for various publishing companies.

Daniel Brennan is a queer writer and coffee devotee from New York. His work has appeared in numerous places, including *Passengers Journal*, *The Banyan Review*, *Birdcoat Quarterly*, and *Sky Island Journal*. He can be found on X and Instagram @dannyjbrennan.

Audra Kerr Brown lives in Iowa. Her short fiction has appeared in *Best Small Fictions* and the *wigleaf* Top 50. Her debut chapbook, *hush hush hush* (2022), is available through Harbor Editions.

JW Burns lives in Florida and has published prose and poetry in several publications, including *I-70 Review*, *Midway Journal*, *ArLiJo*, and *Wilderness House Literary Review*.

Avitus B. Carle lives and writes outside of Philadelphia, Pennsylvania. Formerly known as K.B. Carle, her flash has been published in a variety of places, including *Five South*, *F(r)iction*, *Okay Donkey*, *Lost Balloon*, and elsewhere. It has been selected as one of the 2023 *wigleaf* Top 50, to the *2022 Best of the Net* anthology, and for the *Best Small Fictions 2022* anthology. She can be found at *avitusbcarle.com* or on X @avitusbcarle.

Kevin Carollo has taught world literature and writing at Minnesota State University Moorhead for twenty years and is the author of a chapbook of poems about early-onset dementia, *Elizabeth Gregory* (Rain Taxi/OHM Editions, 2018). His hybrid nonfiction work, *Shred: Running and Being in the End Times*, is forthcoming from North Dakota State University Press.

Christopher Citro is the author of *If We Had a Lemon We'd Throw It and Call That the Sun* (Elixir Press, 2021), winner of the 2019 Antivenom Poetry Award, and *The Maintenance of the Shimmy-Shammy* (Steel Toe Books, 2015). His honors include a 2018 Pushcart Prize for poetry, a 2019 fellowship from the Ragdale Foundation, *Columbia Journal*'s poetry award, and a creative nonfiction *award from The Florida Review*. His poetry appears in *Alaska Quarterly Review*, *The American Poetry Review*, *Denver Quarterly*, *Gulf Coast*, and elsewhere. He lives in Syracuse, New York.

Chloe N. Clark is the author of *Collective Gravities* (Word West, 2020), *Patterns of Orbit* (Baobab Press, 2023), and the forthcoming *Every Galaxy Is a Circle* (JackLeg Press).

Marisa P. Clark is a queer writer whose prose and poetry appear in *Shenandoah*, *Cream City Review*, *Nimrod*, *Epiphany*, and elsewhere. *The Best American Essays 2011* recognized her creative nonfiction among its Notable Essays. She lives in New Mexico.

Maureen Clark is retired from the University of Utah's Department of Writing and Rhetoric Studies, where she taught for 20 years. She served as president of Writers @ Work, editor of *ellipsis... literature and art*, and the director of the University of Utah Writing Center. Her poems have appeared in *Bellingham Review*, *Colorado Review*, *Alaska Quarterly Review*, and *Puerto del Sol*, among other journals.

Lori D'Angelo earned her MFA in creative writing (fiction) from West Virginia University in 2009. She is a grant recipient from the Elizabeth George Foundation, a fellow at the Hambidge Center, and an alumna of the Community of Writers. Recent publications include stories in *Black Moon Magazine*, *Bright Flash Literary Review*, *JAKE*, *Suburban Witchcraft*, and *Worm Moon Archive*.

Daphne Daugherty is a Milwaukee-based poet with an interest in documentary poetics and narrative poetry. Her work has appeared in two anthologies, *Pages Penned in Pandemic* and *Sheltering with Poems*, as well as in *HAD*, *petrichor*, and *Bramble*. She is currently a doctoral candidate in English at the University of Wisconsin-Milwaukee and an associate editor for *Cream City Review*.

Benjamin Davis has poems in literary journals such as *SOFTBLOW*, *Star 82 Review*, and *Maudlin House*, and is the author of the collection *The King of FU* (Nada Blank, 2018). He is now working on his first six novels. He is on X @_benjamin_davis.

Cat Dixon is the author of *What Happens in Nebraska* (Stephen F. Austin University Press, 2022) along with six other poetry chapbooks and collections. She is a poetry editor with *The Good Life Review*. Recent poems have been published in *Book of Matches*, *North of Oxford*, *hex*, and *The Southern Quill*.

Lynn Domina is the author of two collections of poetry, *Corporal Works* (Four Way Books, 1995) and *Framed in Silence* (Main Street Rag, 2011), and the editor of a collection of essays, *Poets on the Psalms* (Trinity University Press, 2011). Her more recent work appears or is forthcoming in *Ninth Letter*, *The Gettysburg Review*, *the museum of americana*, *About Place Journal*, and other periodicals. She is the creative-writing editor of *The Other Journal* and lives in Marquette, Michigan.

Denise Duhamel's most recent books of poetry are *Second Story* (University of Pittsburgh Press, 2021) and *Scald* (University of Pittsburgh Press, 2017). *Blowout* (University of Pittsburgh Press, 2013) was a finalist for the National Book Critics Circle Award. She is a distinguished university professor in the MFA program at Florida International University in Miami.

Coby-Dillon English is a writer from the Great Lakes. A member of the Mississippi Band of Choctaw Indians, they currently are an MFA fiction candidate and Henry Hoyns Fellow at the University of Virginia, where they teach creative writing and serve as the nonfiction editor for *Meridian*. They were a 2023 Tin House Scholar and a 2021 Periplus Collective Fellow. Their writing has appeared or is forthcoming in *Cream City Review*, *Yellow Medicine Review*, and *Salt Hill*.

Jordan Escobar is a writer from central California. He is the author of the chapbook *Men with the Throats of Birds* (CutBank Books, 2023). He is a 2023 winner of the St. Botolph Club Foundation Emerging Artist Award and a 2022 Gregory Djanikian Scholar in poetry. He has been published in many journals, including *Prairie Schooner*, *The Common*, and *The Cortland Review*. He teaches at Emerson College and Babson College.

Shreya Fadia is a Gujarati American writer and former lawyer now based in the mountains of North Carolina. She holds an MFA in creative writing (fiction) from Indiana University, where she served as editor-in-chief of *Indiana Review*. Her recent work has appeared in a handful of publications, including *Black Warrior Review*, *Cream City Review*, *Hobart*, *The Margins*, and the anthology *A Flame Called Indiana* (Indiana University Press, 2023).

Gary Fincke's new collection of flash fiction, *The Corridors of Longing*, was published in 2022 by Pelekinesis Press. The title story was reprinted in *Best Small Fictions 2020*. He is co-editor of the annual anthology *Best Microfiction*.

Jessica Goodfellow's books are *Whiteout* (University of Alaska Press, 2017), *Mendeleev's Mandala* (Mayapple Press, 2015), and *The Insomniac's Weather Report* (Isobar, 2014). A former writer-in-residence at Denali National Park and Preserve, she has had poems in *The Southern Review*, *Ploughshares*, *Scientific American*, *Verse Daily*, and *The Best American Poetry*. She lives in Japan. Find her at *jessicagoodfellow.com*.

Gabrielle Griffis is a musician, writer, and multimedia artist, and she works as a librarian. Her fiction has been published in *wigleaf*, *Split Lip Magazine*, *matchbook*, *Monkeybicycle*, and elsewhere. Her work was selected for *Best Microfiction 2022*. Read more at *gabriellegriffis.com* or follow on X @ggriffiss.

Mary Grimm has had two books published, the novel *Left to Themselves* (Random House, 1993) and the story collection Stealing Time (Random House, 1994), and a number of flash pieces featured in journals such as *Helen*, *The Citron Review*, and *Tiferet*.

Benjamin S. Grossberg's latest book of poems, *My Husband Would* (University of Tampa Press, 2020), won the 2021 Connecticut Book Award in poetry. His other books include *Space Traveler* (University of Tampa Press, 2014) and *Sweet Core Orchard* (University of Tampa Press, 2009), winner of a Lambda Literary Award. He is also the author of a novel, *The Spring Before Obergefell* (University of Nebraska Press, 2024), which won the 2023 AWP Award Series James Alan McPherson Prize for the Novel. He directs the Creative Writing program at the University of Hartford.

Matt Gulley attended Wayne State University in Detroit and the MFA program at Long Island University Brooklyn. He resides in Brooklyn with his partner, Jenna. He has recently been published in *The Madrigal*, *The Twin Bill*, *Blood Tree Literature*, and *The London Reader*. He can be found on X @ selfawareroomba.

Summer Hammond earned her MFA in creative writing (fiction) from the University of North Carolina Wilmington. Her work appears in *The Texas Review*, *Sonora Review*, and *StoryQuarterly*.

Michael Hardin lives in rural Pennsylvania. He is the author of a chapbook, *Born Again*, from Moonstone Press (2019), and has had poems published in *Seneca Review*, *Connecticut Review*, *North American Review*, *Quarterly West*, among other journals.

Andrea Hellman is an associate professor in the English department at Missouri State University, where she specializes in teaching of English to the speakers of other languages. She is also an artist and a member of the

Fresh Gallery and the Formed Gallery in Springfield, Missouri. Her works are available at *andreahellman.com*.

Marcy Rae Henry is a multidisciplinary artist, una Latina/x/e, and an advocate/member of the LGBTQ community. Her writing has received a Chicago Community Arts Assistance Grant, an Illinois Arts Council Agency Fellowship, and first prize in *Suburbia Journal*'s 2021 Novel Excerpt Contest. DoubleCross Press published her chapbook, *We Are Primary Colors* in 2023. She is an associate editor for *RHINO*.

Dustin M. Hoffman is the author of the story collections *One-Hundred-Knuckled Fist* (University of Nebraska Press, 2016) and *No Good for Digging* (Word West, 2019) and the chapbook *Secrets of the Wild* (Word West, 2019). His newest collection, *Such a Good Man*, is forthcoming from University of Wisconsin Press. He teaches creative writing at Winthrop University in South Carolina. His stories have recently appeared in *New Ohio Review*, *Gulf Coast*, *Alaska Quarterly Review*, and *One Story*.

Shen Chen Hsieh is an illustrator, instructor, and art director in Missouri. She studied and graduated with an MFA in the visual study program at Missouri State University. She currently works as an art director in the local design industry.

John Jodzio's work has been featured in *This American Life*, *McSweeney's Internet Tendency*, and *New York* magazine. He is the author of the short-story collections *If You Lived Here You'd Already Be Home* (Catapult, 2017), *Knockout* (Catapult, 2016), and *Get In If You Want To Live* (Paper Darts Press, 2011). He lives in Minneapolis.

Ruth Joffre is the author of the story collection *Night Beast* (Black Cat, 2018). Her work has appeared or is forthcoming in *Lightspeed*, *Nightmare*, *Pleiades*, *khōréō*, and the anthologies *Best Microfiction 2021* and *Best Microfiction 2022*.

Marci Rae Johnson works as an editor for a book publisher. In her previous life, she taught college English. Her poems appear or are forthcoming in *Image*, *Moon City Review*, *The Main Street Rag*, *The MacGuffin*, among other journals. She is the author of two full-length books and one chapbook.

Alex Juffer won the 2022 *Forge* Literary Flash Fiction Competition, and his story was named to the *wigleaf* Top 50 Very Short Fictions for 2023. His work has been previously published in *EPOCH*, *Cleaver*, *Monkeybicycle*, *The Los Angeles Review*, and other journals.

Stephen Lackaye's collection of poems, *Self-Portrait in Dystopian Landscape* (Unicorn Press, 2017), was a finalist for the Oregon Book Award and an Eric Hoffer Book Award. New poems have appeared or are forthcoming in *The Southern Review*, *Southern Indiana Review*, *The Shore*, *Asheville Poetry Review*, and other journals. He lives in Oregon, where he works as a bookseller.

Blair Lee is a queer Japanese American writer who grew up half in the South and half in the Midwest. Her work has appeared in *American Short Fiction*, *The Masters Review Anthology*, and *Bath Flash Fiction*, among other journals. Her scripts have won Scriptapalooza's Television Writing Competition, have been named to the ISA Top 50, and were placed on The Black List's 2021 "Top List." She received her MFA in creative writing from North Carolina State University in 2018.

Eliot Li lives in California. His work appears or is forthcoming in *BULL*, *Juked*, *SmokeLong Quarterly*, *CRAFT*, *Best Small Fictions 2023*, and elsewhere. He was also long-listed for the 2023 *wigleaf* Top 50. He is a submissions editor for *SmokeLong Quarterly*.

Melissa Llanes Brownlee (she/her), a native-Hawaiian writer living in Japan, has work published and forthcoming in *The Rumpus*, *Fractured Lit*, *Gigantic Sequins*, and *Cream City Review* and honored in *Best Small Fictions*, *Best Microfiction*, and the *wigleaf* Top 50. She is also the author of the story collections *Hard Skin* (Juventud Press, 2022) and *Kahi and Lua* (Alien Buddha Press, 2022). Find her on Twitter @lumchanmfa and at *melissallanesbrownlee.com*.

Julia LoFaso's essay is part of a hybrid collection-in-progress. Other pieces from this series have appeared in *Electric Literature*, *The Cincinnati Review*, *Hayden's Ferry Review*, and *The Iowa Review*. Her writing was also selected for the 2021 *wigleaf* Top 50 and *Best Small Fictions 2022* and won *CutBank*'s 2023 Big Sky, Small Prose contest.

Evelyn Maguire is an MFA candidate at the University of Massachusetts Amherst. Her writing can be read or will appear in *Salamander*, *North American Review*, *Cosmonauts Avenue*, and elsewhere.

Abby Manzella is the author of *Migrating Fictions: Gender, Race, and Citizenship in U.S. Internal Displacements*, winner of the Society for the Study of American Women Writers Book Award. She has published in *Literary Hub*, *Colorado Review*, *Catapult*, and *The Threepenny Review* (forthcoming). Find her on X @abbymanzella.

Nicole Markert is a bi/queer poet and educator who recently graduated with their MFA from Rosemont College. Their work has appeared in *Rust & Moth*, *Furrow*, *SWWIM Every Day*, *Glass: A Journal of Poetry*, among other journals. They are also a poetry reader for Saturnalia Books' Poetry Prizes, and they reside in the Philadelphia area while working on their first poetry collection.

Laurie Marshall is a writer, artist, and improv actor. Her debut flash-fiction collection, *Proof of Life*, was released by ELJ Editions in 2023. Her words and art have been published in literary journals and anthologies, including in *Best Small Fictions 2022*. She is a first-year graduate student in the MFA in creative writing program at the University of Arkansas. Find her at *SeeLaurieWrite.com* and on X and Bluesky @LaurieMMarshall.

Ross McMeekin is the author of a novel, *The Hummingbirds* (Skyhorse, 2018). His stories have appeared in magazines and journals such as *Virginia Quarterly Review*, *Shenandoah*, and *Redivider*. He edits the literary journal *Spartan*.

Nathan D. Metz lives in the Bay Area of California. His work has been featured in *The Racket*, *Hawai'i Pacific Review*, *Zaum*, and other journals. He has received scholarships and fellowships from the Elk River Writers Workshop, the Canterbury Program at Santa Clara University, and the AHA.

Will Musgrove is a writer and journalist from northwest Iowa. He received an MFA from Minnesota State University, Mankato. His work has appeared or is forthcoming in *The Penn Review*, *X-R-A-Y Literary Magazine*, *Sundog Lit*, *Tampa Review*, and elsewhere. He is on X at @Will_Musgrove or at *williammusgrove.com*.

Richard Newman is the author of four books of poetry, including the forthcoming *Blues at the End of the World*, and also the novel *Graveyard of the Gods* (Blank Slate Press, 2016). He currently teaches creative writing and world literature at Al Akhawayn University in Morocco. Before moving to the Maghreb, he and his family lived in Vietnam, Japan, and the Marshall Islands.

Derek N. Otsuji is the author of *The Kitchen of Small Hours* (Southern Illinois University Press, 2021), selected by Brian Turner for the Crab Orchard Series in Poetry and featured in *HONOLULU Magazine*'s "Essential Hawai'i Books You Should Read." He is a 2019 Tennessee Williams Scholar and a 2023 Longleaf Fellow in Poetry. Recent work has appeared in *32 Poems*, *The Southern Review*, and *The Threepenny Review*.

Quentin Parker is an undergraduate student at Salisbury University, studying creative writing. He works as a fiction editor and a creative nonfiction associate editor for the university's literary magazine, *Scarab*. He has forthcoming publications in *Hindsight Journal* and *Polaris Literary Magazine*.

Aimee Parkison is the author of several books, including *Refrigerated Music for a Gleaming Woman* (Fiction Collective 2, 2017), winner of the FC2 Catherine Doctorow Innovative Fiction Prize. Parkison teaches in the Creative Writing Program at Oklahoma State University. Her newest book, *Suburban Death Project*, a short story collection, was published by Unbound Edition Press in 2022. More information is available at *aimeeparkison.com*.

Megan Paslawski's short stories have appeared in *Tampa Review*, *Pembroke Magazine*, *The Texas Review*, and elsewhere. She is faculty editor at Lost & Found Press and an assistant professor of English at Queens College, CUNY.

Jason Peck's fiction has appeared or is forthcoming in *SmokeLong Quarterly*, *Jersey Devil Press*, *The Carolina Quarterly*, *X-R-A-Y Literary Magazine*, and *Nothing Short Of: Selected Tales From 100 Word Story*. He lives in Pittsburgh and was a founding editor of *After Happy Hour*.

Meghan Phillips was a 2020 National Endowment for the Arts Literature Fellow, and her short fiction and poems have appeared in *Barrelhouse*, *wigleaf*, *Strange Horizons*, and other publications. Her chapbook, *Abstinence Only*, was published by Barrelhouse Books in December 2020. More about her writing can be found at *meghan-phillips.com*.

Keith J. Powell is co-founder of *Your Impossible Voice* and has recent or forthcoming work in *SoFloPoJo*, *Heavy Feather Review*, *BULL*, *100 Word Story*, and *Does It Have Pockets*. Find more at *keithjpowell.com*.

Jeremy Radin is a writer, actor, teacher, and extremely amateur gardener. His poems have appeared or are forthcoming in *Ploughshares*, *Colorado Review*, *Crazyhorse*, *Gulf Coast*, and elsewhere. He is the author of two collections of poetry: *Slow Dance With Sasquatch* (Write Bloody Publishing, 2012) and *Dear Sal* (Not A Cult, 2022). He is the founder and operator of Lanternist Creative Consulting, through which he coaches writers and performers. He can be found on X @germyradin.

Teresa Buzo Salas is a native of Santa Marta (Badajoz), Spain. After completing her bachelor's degree in Spain, she earned her graduate degree in Hispanic literature at Georgia Southern University, where she now teaches in the Department of World Languages and Cultures. She has authored two novels: *Las hijas de las horas* (Editorial Gregal, 2015) and *Adict@* (Proyecto Argán, 2016). She was the literary reviewer for *Sevilla Actualidad* (Spain) and a columnist for the bilingual monthly *La Voz Latina* (USA).

Austin Sanchez-Moran is a teacher and Pushcart Prize-nominated writer who received his MFA in creative writing (poetry) from George Mason University. His poems and short fiction have been published in *RHINO*, *Denver Quarterly*, and *Salamander*, among many other journals. He has also had poems and short fiction chosen for the anthologies *Best New Poets of the Midwest* (2017) and *Best Microfiction 2020*. His first poetry collection is *Suburban Sutras* (Finishing Line Press, 2021) and his first chapbook, *Rhinocerotica*, was selected as winner of the Backbone Press Chapbook Competition.

Sarah L. Sassone received her doctorate from Binghamton University and holds an MFA from Emerson College. She currently works in the writing departments at Syracuse University and Binghamton University. She has been published in *Monkeybicycle*, *Harpur Palate*, and *Gravel*, among other journals. She can be found at *sarahsassone.com* and on X @sarahsassone.

Autumn Schraufnagel is a creative writing doctoral student at Ohio University. She previously earned an MFA from Oklahoma State University. Her poems have appeared in *North Dakota Quarterly*, *Saw Palm*, *West Trade Review*, *paperbark*, and elsewhere.

Leland Seese's poems appear in *RHINO*, *Stonecoast Review*, *Juked*, *Chestnut Review*, and many other journals. He lives in Seattle with his wife, their six grown children nearby.

Shyla Shehan received an MFA from the University of Nebraska-Lincoln, where she was awarded an Academy of American Poets Prize. Her work has appeared or is forthcoming in *The Midwest Quarterly*, *Drunk Monkeys*, *The Decadent Review*, and elsewhere. She's an editor for *The Good Life Review* and lives in Omaha with her partner and children and can be found at *shylashehan.com*.

Kathryn Silver-Hajo 's story "The Sweet Softness of Dates" was selected for the 2023 *wigleaf* Top 50 longlist. Her work appears in *Atticus Review*, *CRAFT*, *Pithead Chapel*, *Ruby*, and other journals. Her flash collection, *Wolfsong* (ELJ Editions), was published in 2023, and her novel, *Roots of The Banyan Tree* (Flowersong Press), is forthcoming in October. She is at *kathrynsilverhajo.com* and on X @KSilverHajo.

Mary Simmons is a queer poet from Cleveland, Ohio. She is an MFA candidate at Bowling Green State University, where she also serves as an assistant editor for *Mid-American Review*. She has work appearing or forthcoming in *Santa Clara Review*, *The Shore*, *ONE ART*, *tiny wren lit*, and other journals.

Brian Simoneau is the author of the poetry collections *No Small Comfort* (Black Lawrence Press, 2021) and *River Bound* (C&R Press, 2014). His poems have appeared in *Boston Review*, *The Cincinnati Review*, *Colorado Review*, *The Georgia Review*, and other journals. He he lives near Boston with his family.

Dane Slutzky is a queer and trans poet living in western Massachusetts. His poetry has appeared in *Heavy Feather Review*, *Zócalo Public Square*, *LEON Literary Review*, and *Scoundrel Time*. He holds an MFA in poetry from Warren Wilson College and has received support from the Bread Loaf Writers' Conference, Juniper Summer Writing Institute, and Vermont Studio Center.

Jenny Stalter is a writer and former private chef. She was a recipient of a 2023 *SmokeLong Quarterly* Fellowship for Emerging Writers. Her fiction appears in *Longleaf Review*, *Typehouse*, *X-R-A-Y Literary Magazine*, *Ghost Parachute*, and other journals. She is on X @JennyStalter.

Andrew Stancek has been published in *SmokeLong Quarterly*, *Frigg*, *Hobart*, and *Green Mountains Review*, among other journals. He has won contests including the London Independent Story Prize, the Reflex Fiction contest, and the New Rivers Press American Fiction contest.

Kevin Sterne is a writer and painter living in New York state. See more at *kevinsterne.com*.

Thea Swanson holds an MFA in Writing from Pacific University in Oregon and is the founding editor of *Club Plum*. Her anti-Trump flash-fiction collection, *Mars*, was published by Ravenna Press in 2017. Her hybrid essay-and-poem collection, *How To Be a Woman*, was long-listed for the 2021 Dzanc Nonfiction Prize, and her flash-fiction collection, *There and Here*, was longlisted for the 2020 Tarpaulin Sky Book Award.

Laura Valeri is the author of three story collections and a book of literary essays. Her books have won the Iowa Short Fiction Award and the Binghamton University John Gardner Fiction Book Award. Her most recent book, *After Life as a Human*, was a memoir nominee for the Georgia Author of the Year Award. She has an MFA in fiction from the Iowa Writers' Workshop and an MFA in creative writing from Florida International University. She is the founding editor of *Wraparound South*, and she teaches in the undergraduate program at Georgia Southern University.

Anita Vijayakumar is psychiatrist. She has publications in *River Teeth*, *The New York Times'* Tiny Love Stories, HuffPost Personal, and others. She is writing her first novel.

Laura Lee Washburn is the author of *Watching the Contortionists* (Palanquin Chapbook Prize, 1996), *This Good Warm Place* (March Street Press, 1998), *The Book of Stolen Images* (Meadowlark, 2023), and the forthcoming *Arteries* (Pine Row). She has previously published in *Moon City Review* as well as in numerous other literary magazines, including *The Sun* and *SWWIM*. *Harbor Review*'s Washburn Chapbook Prize is named in her honor, and she has been a visiting artist at the Fayetteville Public Library.

Patrick Wilcox studied English and creative writing at the University of Central Missouri, where he also was an assistant editor for *Pleiades* and editor-in-chief of *Arcade*. He is a three-time recipient of the David Baker Award for Poetry, the 2020 honorable mention of *Ninth Letter*'s Literary Award in Poetry, and grand-prize winner of *The MacGuffin*'s Poet Hunt 26. His work has appeared in *Maudlin House*, *Quarter After Eight*, *The Bangalore Review*, and *Copper Nickel*, among other journals. He is a high school teacher.

B. Luke Wilson holds a Bachelor of Arts in English from Virigina Commonwealth University. He served as an intern at *Blackbird* from 2020 to 2023. His work has appeared in *East by Northeast Literary Magazine*, *Virginia Writers Club*, and *Cobblestone*. He won the *Blue Nib* Contest for Fiction in 2020 with the Blue Ridge Writers.

Francine Witte's poetry and fiction have appeared in *SmokeLong Quarterly*, *wigleaf*, *Mid-American Review*, and *Passages North*. Her latest books are *Dressed All Wrong for This* (Blue Light Press, 2019), *The Way of the Wind* (Ad Hoc Fiction, 2020), and *The Theory of Flesh* (Kelsay Books, 2019). She is the flash-fiction editor for *Flash Boulevard* and *SoFloPoJo*. Her flash-fiction chapbook, *The Cake, The Smoke, The Moon*, was published by ELJ Editions in 2021. She lives in New York City.

Kirby Wright holds an MFA in creative writing from San Francisco State University.

Kenton K. Yee's recent poetry appears or is forthcoming in *Rattle*, *The Threepenny Review*, *Constellations*, *Passages North*, and other journals. An Iowa Writers' Workshop Summer Poetry Workshop alumnus, he writes from northern California.